BRIGHT SPOTS FOR DARK DAYS

Mary,
Merry Christmas, 2023!
Stan Blades

Stan Blades

ISBN 978-1-64468-405-4 (Paperback)
ISBN 978-1-64468-406-1 (Digital)

Copyright © 2020 Stan Blades
All rights reserved
First Edition

All rights reserved. No part of this publication may be reproduced, distributed, or transmitted in any form or by any means, including photocopying, recording, or other electronic or mechanical methods without the prior written permission of the publisher. For permission requests, solicit the publisher via the address below.

Covenant Books, Inc.
11661 Hwy 707
Murrells Inlet, SC 29576
www.covenantbooks.com

CONTENTS

Preface...5

Outlook Quotient...7
A Compliment May Alter a Life.............................11
Rainy Days and Mondays Don't Have to Get
You Down..14
The Pursuit of Happiness......................................17
Gratitude: The Antidote for Many Things...............20
Follow Your Heart—Are You Sure About That?.....24
Respect: The Only Way...29
Encouragement: Oxygen to the Soul!.....................33
Just an Old Chunk of Coal? No Way!....................37
You Are What You Read (Listen to and View)........40
HALT...45
Think About It!...48
What's in a Name?..52
Things I Learned from My Mom...........................56
The Best Parenting: Modeling................................61
Leadership: It's About Passion, Judgment,
Communication, and Integrity...............................65
I'm Sorry..71
Maslow Was Partially Correct................................75
The Majesty of God..79
From Coffee to Christ...83

Don't Dispute My Word 87
CULT 92
The Battles Within 98
True Worship 102
Living Life Blindly 107
It's the Message, Not Methods (When It Comes
to Becoming a Christian) 112
Want to Make the World a Better Place? Look in
the Mirror! 116
Your Days Are Numbered 121
His Mercies Are New Every Morning 125
Excuse Me, Can You Tell Me What Is the
Meaning of Life? 128

PREFACE

This work is written from one fellow traveler to another. It is written by a very imperfect human who is still being embraced by the grace of God manifested in Jesus Christ. The following chapters contain truths God has taught me over the years. It is my prayer that God will use these to encourage you and fill you with hope.

I am dedicating this book to my two sons. It is written with them in mind. By the grace of God, they will far exceed the accomplishments of their father. It will only be by His grace that this occurs, for it is only by His grace that anything good is accomplished.

May we experience His grace as we travel onward and impart that same grace to others along the way, for this is what people need above all else.

—Stan Blades

OUTLOOK QUOTIENT

Do you enjoy life? I mean, are you content deep down in your heart of hearts? When you lie down at night to go to sleep, are you at peace? When you get up in the morning, do you look forward to the day with expectation and a sense of mission?

The answer to this question does not depend upon your current economic circumstances, your marital status, or the kind of job you have. All these are external factors. The answer to this question depends mostly upon something inside you. This is *something* everyone possesses, no matter your current circumstances or situation in life. It is also something everyone has control over.

This is reaffirming to know. After all, with changes in the twenty-first century happening at a mind-numbing pace, it is exciting to know you do have control over something. That something is your *outlook*. Your outlook determines the amount of joy, peace, and expectation you have. People have differing amounts of joy, peace, and expectation. To demonstrate this and to determine your outlook quotient, answer the following questions:

- When you wake up each morning, is your attitude one that says, "Good morning, Lord!" or "Good Lord, it's morning?"

- Do you view each day as an opportunity to make a difference in someone else's life?
- During the day, do you view unexpected occurrences or dilemmas as an opportunity to learn and grow, or something to be managed and endured until it goes away?
- Do you view people primarily through a lens of trust or suspicion? In other words, when you first encounter people, do you think the best of them or the worst of them? Are they innocent until proven guilty, or guilty until proven innocent?

The answers to these questions determine to a great extent what your outlook is. Let's take a look at each of these questions.

The answer to the first question determines whether or not you see each new day as a blessing from God and a gift from Him, or whether you see it as something to be lived through, endured, and managed until the evening activities or sleep takes over once again. The "Good morning, Lord" mentality acknowledges that each day is a gift from God. A gift is given to someone whether that someone deserves it or not. A gift is given to someone by someone else who loves them. The first mentality acknowledges this and begins each day with gratitude and a positive outlook. The "Good Lord, it's morning" mentality sees each day as something one has coming to him and displays no gratitude for the gift of life itself. How you begin each day is imperative to your outlook for the rest of the day.

The answer to the second question indicates whether or not you see life as a way to impact the lives of others and the world in a positive way or as all about you. Your answer indicates whether you are primarily a giver or a taker. Givers have more joy because they allow themselves to be poured into others' lives and the world around them. They give their lives to something bigger than themselves and, in so doing, seek to help others, instead of being preoccupied with themselves.

The third question points to how you view life's dilemmas. These may be viewed as problems or opportunities. Unquestionably, life has its difficult circumstances and tragedies. The question is not posed to minimize your need to grieve or work through situations. Certainly, there are stages of grief that must be respected. However, question 3 refers to how you typically view everyday occurrences. If you usually view these occurrences as opportunities in which growth can occur, and something can be learned, then your creativity and passion flows toward successfully navigating to a good place. However, if you see these as problems to be managed, the dread and negativity make the situation worse and make it less likely that you will reach a good place.

The fourth question alludes to your outlook on people. The question does not deny that evil exists in the world and that people often do bad things. It is not meant to imply that one should be naive or unthinking. However, the answer indicates whether a person's first reaction to people is filled with positive or negative energy. Assuming the best of someone is the only fair and right way to live.

If your first thought about someone is one of suspicion and distrust, this sets up an expectation that will likely be fulfilled in your mind, whether or not the impression is grounded in reality. Furthermore, it makes the likelihood of ever having a good relationship with that person highly unlikely. Having this outlook causes you to miss out on having deep friendships with people who may enrich your life.

So how did you do? Do you have a "Good morning, Lord" attitude and one that views each day as an opportunity to make a difference in others' lives? Do you see unexpected occurrences as opportunities to learn? Do you view people with trust and think the best of them? If you answered in the affirmative, you most likely have a positive, can-do, "glass half full" kind of outlook. And you will enjoy reading the rest of this book. If you did not answer these questions in the affirmative, it is likely that your outlook could use some improvement. However, there is good news! Improvement is possible. Not only is it possible, you have control over it. You can choose to start recognizing each day as a gift from God. Embrace your calling to make a difference, view problems as opportunities, and begin to trust people again. I invite you to keep reading and embark on a journey that could be life changing.

A COMPLIMENT MAY ALTER A LIFE

It was my sophomore year of college, and I was a business major. Among the courses I was taking that semester was microeconomics. This was not my favorite course! I had already discovered there was far more to microeconomics than the law of supply and demand. This group of business majors was deep into our grueling, in-depth discovery of economic principles.

This was a quite complicated class, and what made it even more complicated was an overly self-confident professor who loved to tap dance with bells on his shoes. That's right. At the conclusion of a profound point, or when he just wanted to be cute, he would launch into his dance routine. I was not fond of this professor until the day of the group presentation.

I think he felt sorry for the class as he reviewed our averages midway through the semester, so he came up with the group presentation assignment to help improve our grades. The exams he gave were premade exams from the textbook publisher that did not necessarily match the professor's main emphasis, resulting in grades that were nothing to write home about! Each group of students was comprised of two or three underclassmen. I had the privilege of working on my assignment with a pretty and intelligent female classmate.

The day of the presentation came. We had done our research, carefully preparing visual aids for our presentation and making sure we gave correct information, as the watchful eye of the obnoxious professor would be on us. I do not remember much about the presentation itself. However, I do remember what happened at the conclusion.

As you might imagine, there was more nervousness after the presentation than during it, as we would now hear the verdict from the professor. First, he walked over to my classmate and whispered to her what to me were inaudible comments. Then, the moment of truth came for me. I waited for what seemed like an eternity for the professor to then give me his feedback. He stepped toward me and said in a quiet tone, "Anytime you want to teach my class, you let me know," congratulating me on a job well done. Needless to say, I received an A for that presentation.

However, it was not the A that was important. What was important were the words he spoke to me following the presentation. That day, he inspired confidence in me. And his words literally changed the course of my life. From that point forward, I began to think of myself as a teacher and, indeed, eventually changed my major and became a teacher! I have now spent nearly three decades as an educator.

Did the professor know his comments would change the direction of my life? Not likely. Did he make the same comment to most of the students who made a presentation that semester? Maybe. However, his words had tremendous, long-lasting, life-changing impact. And words often do! It really doesn't matter whether the professor made the comment to most of the students. The point is that power resides in the spoken word.

We can use our words for good or evil, healing or harm, encouragement or discouragement, inspiration or desperation. Whatever role you have in your personal or professional life, you have the power to influence with words. Choose carefully. Think before you speak. And above all, realize the power of what you say to another person. It just may change someone's life!

> Let no unwholesome word proceed from your mouth, but only such a word as is good for edification according to the need of the moment, so that it will give grace to those who hear. (Ephes. 4:29)

RAINY DAYS AND MONDAYS DON'T HAVE TO GET YOU DOWN

"Rainy days and Mondays always get me down" are the words of the lovely 1970s singer Karen Carpenter.[1] The song, released in 1971, eventually made it to top of the Billboard charts during that era. Perhaps the lyrics spoke to the way people often felt, or perhaps they were just enamored by her lovely voice. Whatever the reason, it was a song that resonated with people.

This is a sentiment that is often embodied in the day-to-day lives of many people as well. Often, we, as humans, allow circumstances to define our moods and outlook on life. I once knew someone who lived out the sentiments of this song. Mondays were not good days for this individual, and rainy days were even worse. And heaven help us if these two occurred at the same time!

However, this person was not alone in struggling with this issue. Many of us allow factors *outside* ourselves to determine the mood *inside* ourselves. There is no question that some circumstances are indeed daunting. However, to allow uncontrollable factors such as the day of the week or the weather to influence our outlook and behavior is not healthy.

---

[1] Carpenter, Karen, 1971, "Rainy Days and Mondays," *Carpenters*, album.

Let's look at another example. Most of us who work a five-day workweek can't wait until Friday arrives and ushers in the beginning of a two-day hiatus from the grind. Most of us live by the common refrain, "TGIF," or "Thank God it's Friday." When we do this, we effectively eliminate the joy that can be found in day-to-day living. I'm wondering if all of us might enjoy life more if we changed TGIF to TGIN—Thank God it's Now. If we would simply treasure the very moment in which we live, we would be able to drink deeply from the well of living.

Scripture has much to say about day-to-day living. Psalm 118:24 says, "This is the day which the Lord has made; Let us rejoice and be glad in it." First, we notice that it is God who allows us to be a part of each day. Therefore, there should be a grateful attitude toward the One whose "mercies never come to an end" [Lam. 3:22]. When we see each day as a gift from God, our attitude will be one of appreciation even if it is a Monday!

Now let's turn to the rain. Jesus, the Son of God, said in the often-quoted Sermon on the Mount that God "sends rain on the righteous and the unrighteous" (Matt. 5:45). A rainy day should not be a personal affront to anyone, as God allows the rain to impact all types of people. The rain is not bad in and of itself. Therefore, we should not allow it to ruin our day.

Specific days and weather conditions are only two of the many factors we often allow to impact us in a negative way. Perhaps someone cuts us off in traffic or the clerk at the convenience store is rude to us. We can *choose* to internalize these incidents and stew over them, or we can consider the possibility that the person committing these discourtesies is allowing external factors of his own to impact how he behaves toward other people and not take it personally. This indeed is a *choice* we make. When we choose to allow the discourtesies of others to impact our behavior, we allow a cycle of negativity to continue and continue to perpetuate rudeness in the world. Conversely, when we consider the needs of the other person and determine not to allow his behavior to affect ours, the cycle of rudeness stops with us.

The real issue with all of the above is an overdependence upon emotions being influenced by factors outside of ourselves. We need to pray for the inner peace only God can provide. Once He gives us the "peace that passes understanding," we are on the road to stability *within* and the promotion of peace and goodwill *without*.

THE PURSUIT OF HAPPINESS

"We hold these truths to be self-evident that all men are created equal, that they are endowed by their Creator with certain inalienable rights, that among these are Life, Liberty, and the pursuit of Happiness."[2] We, of course, recognize these words penned by Thomas Jefferson in the United States Declaration of Independence from Great Britain. Through the decades, these words have had tremendous impact on the lives of most Americans. They speak of equality and God-given rights, valuable tenets of what it means to be an American.

Have you ever taken the time to really think about what happiness really means? Most everyone wants to be happy. After all, isn't life all about finding happiness? The *Online Etymology* dictionary tells us "a great majority of the European words for *happy* at first meant *lucky*. An exception is Welsh, where the word first meant *wise*."[3] So is happiness about pursuing luck or wisdom? How do you pursue luck? If you believe in luck, isn't it just something that happens *to* you instead of something you pursue? And what about wisdom? Is wisdom something that can be gained by

---

[2] Jefferson, Thomas. "The Declaration of Independence." 1776.
[3] "Happy (adj.)," *Online Etymology Dictionary*, accessed November 23, 2019, https://www.etymonline.com/word/happy.

pursuit or is it a gift? Knowledge can certainly be obtained by pursuing it through education, reading, and research, but is knowledge the same as wisdom? And does wisdom bring happiness?

Merriam-Webster defines happiness as "as state of well-being and contentment or a pleasurable or satisfying experience."[4] If happiness is a state or circumstance, what happens to your level of contentment when circumstances change? Perhaps happiness can be found in a relationship with someone. However, what happens when that relationship ends? Maybe happiness is found when you put food, drink, or substance into your body, but what happens when the effects of that substance dissipate? Perhaps a career or finances can ensure happiness. What if the economy turns south, and that career ends, and along with it, the finances? We can conclude from pondering these questions that happiness is a temporary condition dependent on outward circumstances. So is it wrong to pursue happiness? Not necessarily, as long we realize that it may only be temporary. It is an undeniable fact that life is quite uncertain. As long as we hold this truth as self-evident, then happiness may be pursued, however elusive it may be.

It is almost as if the harder you try to be happy, and the more experiences you seek, the less happiness you find. The apostle Paul of the first century wrote that he had learned to be content whatever the circumstances. Notice that he said that he *learned*. It did not come naturally. You have to understand that Paul was a very educated man of his day. He had also been a very powerful man with authority over

---

[4] "Happiness noun," *Merriam-Webster*, accessed November 23, 2019, https://www.merriam-webster.com/dictionary/happiness.

many of his Jewish contemporaries. Following his conversion, he became one of the most influential figures of the early Christian church, with many people who held him in high esteem and displayed great affection for him, as can be seen when he left Ephesus after three years of ministry there. However, even with all this, he had to learn contentment.

Perhaps, he had to learn it because he was imprisoned numerous times for proclaiming his faith. Furthermore, he was shipwrecked, stoned, beaten, and left for dead. How could anyone who had been through so many highs and lows in life say he had learned to be content? The aforementioned circumstances are historical facts. They really happened to Paul, and he really wrote that he had learned to be content. What was his secret? It really is no secret because he followed his statement by saying "I know how to get along with humble means, and I also know how to live in prosperity; in any and every circumstance I have learned the secret of being filled and going hungry... I can do all things through Him who strengthens me" (Phil. 4:12–13). The *him* that Paul was referring to was Jesus Christ.

Perhaps you already are a believer and follower of Jesus, but you sense that contentment is just not what characterizes your life. Will you consider reading or rereading the writings of the apostle Paul to see how you can discipline yourself to be content? Philippians would be a good book with which to begin. Read it and reread it, allowing the truths of God's word to teach you. Happiness may be pursued, but it is better to pursue joy and contentment that will not be taken away in this life or in eternity. Enjoy the journey!

GRATITUDE: THE ANTIDOTE FOR MANY THINGS

In the New Testament, in 1 Thessalonians, the apostle Paul writes "In everything give thanks; for this is God's will for you in Christ Jesus" (Thess. 5:18). Wow! Paul, writing under the inspiration of the Holy Spirit, tells us we are to be grateful no matter what is going on around us! This can be a tough pill to swallow, as there are some very difficult circumstances in life. Disease, famine, and death of a loved one—these, among others, are situations in which it is difficult to apply what the word of God is asking us to do. However, the word of God is true and expresses God's desire for how we should live our lives to bring glory to Him. Therefore, we must look at this verse more carefully to examine what it is telling us.

First, let's take a look at the preposition *in*. Notice what the verse does *not* say. The verse does not say we should give thanks *for* all circumstances. There are circumstances like the ones mentioned above, which we really cannot give thanks *for* them. The preposition *in* indicates what our attitude should be within any circumstance or situation in life. This means that whatever circumstances within which we operate, we should not forget to look up and give thanks to God for His grace.

This is true for both the good times and the bad. We are prone to forget to give thanks to God in both situations. We often do not acknowledge the blessings of God in the good times. We must remember that "every good thing given and every perfect gift is from above, coming down from the Father of lights, with whom there is no variation or shifting shadow" (James 1:17). All the blessings we enjoy—the gift of life; daily necessities; the love of spouse, child, parent; etc.—come from God. Without His sustaining power, presence, and love, none of these would be possible. It is because of the presence of God in the world that any good takes place. This is epitomized in the old Amy Grant song "Hope Set High," when she sings, "If there's anything good that happens in life, it's from Jesus."[5]

One can understand this during good times, but what about the bad? I once heard about a young widow who was grieving over the death of her young husband. His life had been cut short by cancer. One would expect devastation at a time like this, and one could certainly understand it if the young widow had expressed anger, but she did neither of these. Instead, when someone expressed sympathy for her great loss, she simply stated she was grateful for the time she had with him. This is incredible! Notice the focus of this young lady. The focus was not on what time she would lose with her spouse because they could not spend the rest of their lives together. Instead, her focus was on the time she did have with him. This is the epitome of gratitude. Gratitude focuses on what one has been given instead of what one does not have.

---

[5] Grant, Amy, 1990, "Hope Set High," *Heart in Motion*, album.

When we do this, no matter the circumstance, this increases our contentment level. Discontented people focus on what they do not have. There is restlessness within someone who is always longing for more. They want just one more thing, just one more experience, just one more minute. Conversely, contented people have learned to focus on the blessings they have been given, period. End of story.

In 1 Thessalonians 5:18, the phrase "give thanks" is the Greek word *eucharisteo*, and it literally means "good grace" or "properly, acknowledging that God's grace works well."[6] Therefore, we are to acknowledge God's good grace *in* all circumstances, even during times of grief. While this is certainly not easy, by God's grace, a person can find strength to develop the perspective that God's grace works well.

Finally, we notice that 1 Thessalonians 5:18 concludes by stating "For this is God's will for you in Christ Jesus." All of Scripture presents the will and ways of God. However, there are not many times that we read explicitly "for this is the will of God." It is clear in this verse that having a grateful attitude in all situations of life is the will of God for each believer and follower of Christ. While we may be uncertain of God's specific will in particular situations in life, we can always be certain that no matter the situation His preferred will for us is that we be thankful toward Him for His good grace works well.

The object of gratitude must be God from whom all blessings flow. We are not to have gratitude just because it is the right attitude. Gratitude must be expressed to some-

---

[6] "Strong's Concordance," Biblehub.com, accessed November 23, 2019, https://biblehub.com/greek/2168.htm.

one, and the proper expression is to the One who oversees all of life's circumstances, the Sovereign Lord. Gratitude is giving credit to whom credit is due. If you do something for me, the appropriate response from me is to thank you. On a much higher scale, this is true for Almighty God, who sustains our lives by his very power "for in Him we live and move and exist" (Acts 17:28).

Gratitude toward God is something that delights Him. In Luke 17, we read the account of Jesus traveling along the border between Samaria and Galilee. While traveling, He encountered ten lepers who asked for healing. He gave them instructions to go and present themselves to the priest, and as they went they were healed. Only one of ten took the time to turn and acknowledge Jesus for what He had done, "and he fell on his face at His feet, giving thanks to Him" (v. 16). Jesus's response was "Were not ten cleansed? But the nine—where are they? Was no one found who returned to give glory to God, except this foreigner?" (v. 17–18).

All ten had been healed of a terrible, ostracizing disease that made them socially unacceptable. Jesus had freed them from the pain of the disease, and now, they could interact freely with others in society. But only one of the ten took the time to say "thank you" to the Son of God who had healed them. May you be found among the minority in society today who take the time to offer thanksgiving and praise to God on a regular basis. The Father delights in this! It is the Father's will, and you will find immeasurable contentment as you express gratitude to Him!

FOLLOW YOUR HEART—ARE YOU SURE ABOUT THAT?

In today's society, we are often told to follow our heart. This is especially true in relationships with other people. We hear this sentiment in the lyrics of modern-day songs and see it played out on TV, in the movies, and on the internet. Dionne Warwick sings, "Never trust your dreams when you're about to fall in love. For your dreams may quickly fall apart so if you're smart, really smart only trust your heart."[7] However, we must ask ourselves if what we are seeing and hearing is reality and based on truth. We must not be passive consumers of sights and information without processing what we are viewing. The late Steve Jobs said, "Follow your heart, but check it with your head."[8] Someone else said, "follow your heart, but take your brain with you."[9]

First, to determine whether or not the above advice from contemporary figures is sound, we must examine what

---

[7] Warwick, Dionne, "Only Trust Your Heart," Track 8 *Only Trust Your Heart,* 1995, album.
[8] "Quote," AZ Quotes, accessed November 23, 2019, https://www.azquotes.com/quote/1060061.
[9] "Quote," Goodreads, accessed November 23, 2019, https://www.goodreads.com/quotes/623973-follow-your-heart-but-take-your-brain-with-you.

Scripture says about the heart and its condition. The word *heart* (Greek *kardia*) is mentioned more than eight hundred times in Scripture, but "it never refers to the literal physical pump that drives the blood."[10] When you see the word *heart* in the Bible, it is referring to "the affective center of our being and the capacity of moral preference, the desire producer that makes us tick," and the unique combination of "desire-decisions that establish who we are."[11]

Let's look first in the Old Testament, in the book of Jeremiah, to discover the condition of the heart. In Jeremiah 17:9, the prophet writes "The heart is more deceitful than all else and is desperately sick; Who can understand it?" Now, this does not paint a picture of something that should be followed or even trusted. The Hebrew meaning of the word *deceitful* is "crooked, deceitful and polluted."[12] These are not adjectives that describe a source that can be trusted with life's most precious decisions. How many of us would trust someone known to be a crooked or deceitful individual? Many politicians have lost their credibility and careers over deceitful actions. Now, if we wouldn't trust leaders who display deceit, why would we trust our own heart, which is prone to deceitfulness. We must not fool ourselves into thinking that just because it's *our* heart, and not some other person or outside source, that we can always trust what our heart tells us. It's just not true. We cannot always

---

[10] "Strong's Concordance," Biblebub.com, accessed November 23, 2019, https://biblehub.com/greek/2588.htm.

[11] Strong's Concordance," Biblebub.com, accessed November 23, 2019, https://biblehub.com/greek/2588.htm.

[12] "Strong's Exhaustive Concordance," Biblehub.com, accessed November 23, 2019, https://biblehub.com/hebrew/6121.htm.

trust our hearts, which is why Jobs said to use our brains as well.

What did Jesus say concerning the condition of the human heart? Jesus said, "For out of the heart come evil thoughts, murders, adulteries, fornications, thefts, false witness, slanders. These are the things which defile the man; but to eat with unwashed hands does not defile the man" (Matt. 15:19–20). The Pharisees and scribes had just come to Jesus inquiring as to why Jesus's disciples ate with unwashed hands, not observing the ritual washing of Jewish tradition, and this was Jesus's response. Jesus, the author and embodiment of truth, identified that the sins people commit originate in the heart. In light of this, we must take serious pause before we live our lives trusting our hearts in all situations.

In fact, Proverbs offers this strong admonition "Watch over your heart with all diligence, for from it flow the springs of life." In contrast to saying, "Follow your heart," the writer of Proverbs says *"guard* your heart." Ancient wisdom tells us to keep watch over our hearts. We are to guard the inner man, and the Hebrew concept of the inner man is the mind, will, and the heart. We are given the reason in this verse regarding why it is vital to guard our hearts, and that is because it determines the course of our lives. As the heart goes, so goes the man and woman. The heart acts as a compass, steering the direction of our lives. Given the fact that the heart is prone to deceit and sinful desires, we are to hold it in check by keeping watch over it.

This keeping watch is a constant task. Another translation of Scripture says we are to guard our hearts with all *dil-*

igence. The Hebrew word here is *mishmar*, and it means "a place of confinement or jail."[13] We are to guard our hearts much as a prison guard would guard a dangerous prisoner in order to prevent escape. In reality, this is what we are trying to prevent. We are seeking to prevent the desires of the heart from spiraling out of control. The danger in a prisoner escaping is that he/she would do further harm to society, wreaking havoc on the lives of others. This is what a human heart living outside the boundaries God has established can do—bring destruction to one's own life and the lives of other people.

You argue most people have a good heart. That is the prevalent thinking in society. This type of thinking says that most people have a good nature and want to do what is in the best interest of others. One of our country's founding fathers, Thomas Jefferson, even said, "Morality, compassion, generosity are innate elements of the human constitution" (Letter to Pierre-Samuel Du Pont, 24 April 1826).[14] However, this runs counter to what Scripture says. We must allow Scripture to define reality instead of current thinking on a subject or someone's opinion about the human heart. We must trust the very God who created us and who inspired scriptural truth to define reality for us and instruct us on how to live our lives.

We must do whatever it takes to bring our desires under the control of the Holy Spirit, who lives within every person whom Christ Jesus has redeemed. We must, in essence,

---

[13] "Strong's Concordance," Biblehub.com, accessed November 23, 2019, https://biblehub.com/hebrew/4929.htm.
[14] Jefferson, Thomas, 1826, "Letter to Pierre-Samuel Du Pont," April 24, 1826.

do what is necessary to guard our hearts. Our children, spouses, churches, society, and even ourselves will benefit from keeping our hearts in check and living for the glory of the God who made us.

RESPECT: THE ONLY WAY

Respect is one of the essential missing ingredients in society today. We would be naive to believe people could coexist without disagreements. It is a given that people will have differing perspectives, outlooks, and beliefs; and arguments or discussions, however you would like to characterize them, are inevitable. However, the factor each person has control over is the manner in which those arguments are conducted. The missing ingredient in most moral, social, and political arguments today is that people on both sides of issues do not respect one another. You can hear it in the words they speak to one another and see it in their body language. Many people are dug in so deeply to their cause they feel that if they demonstrated respect for one another, this would be a compromise.

We see this being played out on the political battlefields within the United States. We have red states and blue states, Republicans and Democrats, conservatives and liberals. Our country's first president warned about the matters that would seek to divide us. George Washington said:

> The alternate domination of one faction over another, sharpened by the spirit of revenge, natural to party dissension,

which in different ages and countries has perpetrated the most horrid enormities, is itself a frightful despotism. But this leads at length to a more formal and permanent despotism. The disorders and miseries, which result, gradually incline the minds of men to seek security and repose in the absolute power of an individual; and sooner or later the chief of some prevailing faction, more able or more fortunate than his competitors, turns this disposition to the purposes of his own elevation, on the ruins of Public Liberty.[15]

We also see this type of division within Christianity with a plethora of denominations, when the world would be better served by Christians emphasizing what we agree on as opposed to what divides us. Families see this happening when husbands and wives view their differences in personality and preferences as matters on which to "claim the hill and die on," instead of matters for which to love and appreciate the uniqueness of one another.

If we could view one another with the truth that each person is made in the image of God and then treat each person accordingly, respect could permeate everything we say and do. However, we must first agree on this basic truth. God said "Let us make man in our image" (Gen.

---

[15] "Quote," Goodreads, accessed November 23, 2019, https://www.goodreads.com/quotes/158945-the-alternate-domination-of-one-faction-over-another-sharpened-by.

1:26). Scripture goes on to say "God created man in his own image, in the image of God he created him" (Gen. 1:27). Three times in the very first chapter of the Bible, we are told God created humans in His own image.

At least two truths are important here. First, the Bible does not say that humans are God. It does not say God created "little gods." This is important to realize. The reason this is important is that since we are not God, there is no possible way for us to have all the information, knowledge, or insight that only God has about individuals. There is no possible way we can tell what is running through a person's mind or from what motives the person is being propelled. Indeed, some operate from selfish, and even evil, motives. However, we must leave the judgment of those selfish and evil motives to God. And be sure that He alone is qualified to render perfect judgment, and He will indeed do that. Paul wrote to the church at Rome and said "Beloved, never avenge yourselves, but leave it to the wrath of God, for it is written, 'Vengeance is mine, I will repay, says the Lord'" (Rom. 12: 19).

Secondly, the Bible does say humans have been created in God's likeness. Each human has been created to resemble God. Therefore, when we disrespect another human being by the way we treat them, we are disrespecting the holy, omniscient God who made them. Everyone from Wall Street to Main Street would do well to remember this!

One might challenge this truth by saying that certain people do not behave in ways that reflect the image of God. This is true. When any one of us exhibit immoral behavior, we behave in ways that God is not pleased, and we disrespect the very God who put His image within us. However, no matter how immoral one has been, that person still retains the image of God, even though that image has been greatly marred. The challenge in our day is to be able to see through all of each other's behaviors and get to the image of God in a person.

Proverbs 22:2 gets to the heart of the matter. Solomon writes "The rich and poor have this in common: The Lord made them both." It is not our wealth or lack thereof that defines our worth. It is the fact that God makes each individual who is conceived and born into this world. We should have respect for each person God has made. This is where respectful dialogue concerning important issues begins. There are many other skills involved in having respectful dialogue. Skills such as intentional listening while not thinking about our response and phrasing one's own perspective in ways that do not antagonize are important skills. These begin with the correct view of the other person as being worth listening to and interacting with simply because that person is a creation of God. As the old saying goes, "God don't make no junk."

Let's begin respectful dialogue in our families, churches, communities, courthouses and legislatures by valuing each person as a treasure of God! God will honor those who "give preference to one another in honor" (Rom. 12:10) to others and who "so far as it depends on them, be at peace with all men" (Rom. 12:18).

ENCOURAGEMENT: OXYGEN TO THE SOUL!

I can live for two months on a good compliment.
—Mark Twain

I think we underestimate the great need that people have for encouragement in the twenty-first century. While the old song says, "What the world needs now is love, sweet love,"[16] and I would not necessarily disagree with this, what we need in equivalent doses is encouragement. In some respect, we live in a hopeless age. Consider this, "In 2016, suicide became the second leading cause of death for ages 10–34 and the fourth leading cause for ages 35–54."[17]

At a time, early in life, when young people should have the most hope many are struggling with huge burdens and some succumb terminally under the weight of these burdens. While we could spend our time debating the causes of such hopelessness, let's focus instead on a strategy to help this lack of hope. One such strategy is encouragement.

---

[16] Jackie DeShannon, "What the World Needs Now," *This is Jackie DeShannon,* 1965, album.
[17] "Suicide Mortality in the United States, 1999–2017," Centers for Disease Control and Prevention, accessed November 24, 2019, https://www.cdc.gov/nchs/products/databriefs/db330.htm.

Now, please understand, I am not suggesting that if we all become encouragers suicide will go away. However, I am suggesting that if we deliberately choose to be an encouraging influence in the lives of people, people will have greater hope and will become less likely to succumb to a spirit of hopelessness.

We need to become *hope dispensers* in the lives of people. We need to become vessels of encouragement who pour into the lives of other people. Consider the word derivation of *encouragement*. It comes from the French word *encoragier,* meaning "make strong, hearten."[18] In essence, an encourager is someone who puts courage into another person. An encourager pours into someone else what that someone may not have or may not think they have within their own capacity or resources. It's what parents, teachers, pastors, leaders, mentors, and grandparents do.

Far too often, humans beat up on themselves on the inside. People who may seem they totally have it together on the outside may struggle considerably with negative voices on the inside, telling themselves they do not measure up. I personally believe this may be a strategy of the evil one in this world to actively keep people from reaching their God-given potential. As encouragers, we can speak truth into people's lives as we relay to them what they may not see in themselves. By doing so, we may just change the trajectory of another person's life.

However, in order to be a person of encouragement, a hope dispenser, we must commit to taking the focus off

---

[18] "Encourage," Vocabulary.com, accessed November 24, 2019, https://www.vocabulary.com/dictionary/encourage.

ourselves and our own needs and look deeply into other people to see their needs. It is then that we begin to become interested in someone other than ourselves and to pour into their lives. An amazing thing happens as we do this. We find *ourselves* being filled with hope and purpose, as we become others-centered and dispensers of the hope *they* desperately need.

It's what Barnabas did in the first century Christian church. Now, we know him as Barnabas, but his real name was Joseph. Barnabas was a nickname that meant "son of encouragement." Barnabas believed in people for whom others had great doubts. Consider what he did for the apostle Paul. Before Paul became a Christian, he was a persecutor of Christians, to the point of authorizing their deaths. Following his conversion, one can understand how early Christ followers would be skeptical of someone who now said he had become one of them, but had previously killed their fellow believers. Barnabas, however, saw in Paul what others did not see. The book of Acts declares "And when he [Paul] came to Jerusalem, he was trying to associate with the disciples; but they were all afraid of him, not believing that he was a disciple" (Acts 9: 26). When no one else was willing to take a chance on Paul, Barnabas took a chance. Have you ever considered how the world might be different today had Barnabas not taken a chance on Paul? Three missionary journeys, the spread of the gospel, and thirteen New Testament books could be absent from Christian history! Barnabas saw in Paul what others did not see, and as a result, the course of untold numbers of lives have been changed throughout the centuries.

Now, I realize Jesus Christ was actually the One who changed untold numbers of lives. However, He used Paul, the apostle, to be the herald of His good news, and Barnabas acted on Christ's behalf to speed this along. And we, too, can be "Barnabases" to those with whom we rub elbows. God made each of us relational creatures to pour into the lives of others. There are people in your sphere of influence that need encouragement today. Be sensitive to the needs of those around you. Look deeply into their eyes and see the need, and then pour courage into their lives. It may be just what they need to make it through the day or the impetus for a lifetime of greatness in the kingdom of God.

JUST AN OLD CHUNK OF COAL? NO WAY!

A number of years ago, 1981 to be exact, country singer John Anderson recorded the song "I'm Just an Old Chunk of Coal."[19] The idea in the song is that the person is currently just a chunk of coal, but through prayer, kindness, and lots of effort, the person would one day become a diamond. It's an interesting concept.

However, scientists tell us the chances of a chunk of coal becoming an actual diamond are slim to none. It seems that diamonds are formed much deeper beneath the earth's surface than coal. In fact, the two substances are not even close in proximity to one another beneath the earth's surface. It sure makes a catchy tune though.

The song also conveys an important concept to keep in mind when encountering others. Whether it's a child, student, coworker, fellow churchgoer, or distant relative, we could learn something from this fictional transformation process of coal to diamond. How you view another person is critical in that person's development process, especially if you interact with that person on a regular basis.

---

[19] Anderson, John, 1981, "I'm Just an Old Chunk of Coal (But I'm Gonna Be a Diamond Someday)," *John Anderson 2*, album.

You see, to a great extent, we live up to the expectations of other people. We often see it with children. Over time, children will live up or down, whichever the case may be, to the expectations of the adults in their lives. You will notice that I said "over time." Scientists tell us that if a chunk of coal could ever possibly become a diamond, it would take place over an extremely long time. By the same token, when I discuss the transformation of people in the following paragraphs, I understand that the transformation often takes place over years.

However, transformation can and does take place in a person's life, often through someone else believing in that person, even when that person did not believe in himself/herself. How many athletes have become successful because a coach chose to believe in them even when they didn't play their best? How many writers, doctors, ministers, plumbers, investors, politicians, performers are successful today because someone saw them as a diamond, even when they were merely a chunk of coal? How many children grow up to be successful, contributing, citizens of integrity because their parents refused to give up on them? On the other hand, how many people sit in jail today because no one took the time earlier in their lives to value them as people and believe that they were capable individuals?

Each of us has a contribution to make to the lives of other people. There are people that God has put within our spheres of influence. It is up to us whether or not we will make a positive difference in their lives. However, the difference will not be made by chance. Each of us must make a conscious effort to see into the lives of other people and become involved in a meaningful way. We do not have to change the world to make a significant contribution to it. We can choose to make that contribution simply by making the choice to treat each person whom we come into contact with as someone having great worth, a diamond, if you will. Simply making this attitude adjustment is a start.

Once this adjustment is made, a kind word, a genuine smile, or a pat on the back can go a long way toward speaking worth into people's lives. We need to be *worth dispensers*. What if only a million people decided to make this conscious decision to dispense worth into the lives of other individuals? This could start an entire wave of kindness that could revolutionize much of society! Someone may say, "This is too pie in the sky! This is only the ideal, but not reality." Correct, this is not reality, because so many people do *not* make the deliberate choice to treat others with dignity and respect. However, reality can be changed when people make the choice to treat others as a diamond. The ripple effect of people choosing to do this could be dramatic.

This could inspire greatness in others, a cure for cancer, a drop in teenage pregnancy, less crime, and the list goes on and on. You never know when you may be the only inspiration someone has. Take the step. Make the choice. Treat each person with whom you come into contact with not as a chunk of coal, but as a diamond. The person may currently be a chunk of coal, but that same person will never have the chance to become a diamond, unless someone else treats them like one. Where would you be today if someone hadn't believed in you?

YOU ARE WHAT YOU READ (LISTEN TO AND VIEW)

*N*BC News reported the findings of a research study about the effects reading has on a person's thinking. These researchers found "when you lose yourself in a work of fiction, your behavior and thoughts can metamorphose to match those of your favorite character."[20] On the one hand, this is great news, if your favorite character is a positive one.

On the other hand, what if your character is a serial killer? This is what Geoff Kaufman, one author of the study, alluded to when he said about one main character in a modern-day novel, "the character is very likable and charismatic. But he's a serial killer. To the extent that you connect with him, you may try to understand or justify the actions he's committing."[21]

Kaufman and his coauthor, Lisa Libby, call the process of taking on your "favorite character's emotions, thoughts and beliefs 'experience-taking.'"[22] They "found that experi-

---

[20] "You Are What You Read, Study Suggests," NBC News, accessed November 28, 2019, https://www.nbcnews.com/health/body-odd/you-are-what-you-read-study-suggests-flna769363.
[21] Ibid.
[22] Ibid.

ence-taking can lead to real changes in the lives of readers."[23] Finally, research confirms what has long been known. You are what you read, or as the authors of the study might say, you are *whom* you read.

You have often heard it said, "You are what you eat." The idea, of course, is that if you put healthy foods into your body, then you are healthy, and the opposite of this is true as well. Not many people would dispute this decades-old phrase concerning food and its link to a person's health. Neither should we have difficulty understanding the impact of our reading upon our mental health and outlook on life. Show me a person who reads mostly gloom and doom, and I will show you a person with a negative attitude. On the other hand, take a person who reads mostly positive, uplifting material, and you will most likely have a person with a positive outlook on life.

Another way of saying this is "Garbage in, garbage out." This phrase is often used in computer circles to indicate that bad data put into a program will yield bad results. The phrase is also used in the manufacturing world to say that if you use poor quality materials to create a product, you will get a poor product in the end. The phrase can also refer to what we read. If we read only lies, gossip, hopeless forecasts, and half-truths, then eventually, we will start to believe what we read. The mind has an uncanny way of conforming to what we put into it.

These truths are not new. Ancient wisdom literature teaches us "for as he thinks within himself, so he is" (Prov. 23:7). We become like our thoughts. In Hebrew thinking,

---

[23] Ibid.

when the "heart" was referred to, it carried with it the idea of a person's whole self, including the mind. Therefore, it should be no surprise to find the following: "Watch over your heart with all diligence, for from it flow the springs of life" (Prov. 4:23). It is vital we carefully choose what to put into our minds by way of reading.

This is true not only with what we read, but also with what we listen to in the way of music. Music has long been known to have a powerful influence on people. Certain melodies can create certain moods in us. An upbeat, lively tune can bring joy to our spirit, and a slow song in a minor key can lead to sadness. However, the impact of music is far greater when we put lyrics in the mix. Over time, we conform to the lyrics we hear on a consistent basis. For example, let us say that a young man consistently listens to music that justifies sleeping around with various women in his pursuit of happiness. Eventually, the young man may begin to act on the thoughts he consistently hears on the radio.

The formation of his character and actions does not happen in a day. It is not that the young man sets out to behave in this way. It is that he has developed thought patterns *over a long period of time* that have been partially formed by what he listened to. If all he ever listens to are songs with unwholesome messages, and there are no positive counter influences in his life, he will eventually act on what he has come to believe as truth as a result of what he hears and reads.

Now let us turn to the powerful influence that visual stimuli have on us. Psychologists tell us that no visual image is ever lost. Visual images are forever stored in our brains. One may not have immediate access to each of these images. However, these images are stored in our mental database and greatly influence our approach to people, circumstances, and life, in general. For example, let's say a young man or young woman consistently views pornography. These images are seared into the brain and have the potential to impair future relationships with the opposite sex.

He may not realize that viewing pornography degrades humanity in a way that views the opposite sex as merely someone to give physical pleasure. It causes one to not focus as much on the more important aspects of a person, such as values, thoughts, attitudes, and personality. In this way pornography causes him to have skewed and unrealistic expectations of every person with whom he tries to develop a meaningful relationship. The same is true for viewing television programs, movies, or anything that causes him to be a spectator of an event that is meant to take place in privacy between a husband and wife.

Reading material, music, and visual media all have a powerful influence on a person's psyche. This influence is true for adults, but it is especially impacting on adolescents. "More than one-thousand scientific studies and reviews conclude that significant exposure to violent music and lyrical content increase the risk of aggressive behavior in certain children and adolescents. The explicit lyrics desensitize the listener and give the impression that the world is a meaner place than it really is."[24] This desensitization

---

[24] Committee on Public Education 1998–1999, "Media Education," *American Academy of Pediatrics,* accessed November 28, 2019, https://pediatrics.

effectively redefines reality, causing adolescents to view as "normal" what is abnormal behavior.

This is a clear call to parents to monitor what their children listen to and view. It is also a clear call to present adolescents with the facts. Many adolescents will not venture into something if they know it is bad for them. When educated about the impact of what they put into their brains via the senses, many adolescents will make wiser choices *when they realize what is best for them*. We must have greater confidence in young people. Not every young person is set on being bad. The truth is that many of them will choose the right path *when shown the way* by parents, teachers, and other adults in their lives. We have the power to choose what to put into our minds and the influence to persuade others to digest healthy mental thoughts and images as well. Whose mental health will you influence today?

---

aappublications.org/content/pediatrics/104/2/341.full.pdf

HALT

H—Am I Hungry?
A—Am I Angry?
L—Am I Lonely?
T—Am I Tired?

The above acrostic has been used in psychology, religion, and Alcoholics Anonymous. The idea is that if you overreact to something and act in ways that are not typical, you need to ask yourself the above four questions. If the answer is yes to any one of the four questions, it just may be this unmet human need is the culprit contributing to making a tough situation even tougher.

Can you imagine how many harsh words or actions have been fueled by the fact that one's basic needs are not being met? Self-care is an often overlooked area in one's life. This is especially true if one has an inner compulsion to overactivity and a drive to excel that has overtaken one's life. However, when we fail to take care of ourselves, we not only harm ourselves, but potentially others as well.

"But taking care of myself is selfish," you may say! Really? So answer this question. If you are on an airplane, in a situation where the oxygen masks deploy, whose face are you going to affix the oxygen mask to first? Yours or your child beside you? You place it on your face first, so you will have the oxygen you need in order to have the alertness to place the mask on your child. You see, you can't take care of your child until you take care of yourself first. The same principle applies to self-care. We must take good care of ourselves in order to be able to help others.

Jesus commands "You shall love your neighbor as yourself" (Mark 12:31). How can you effectively love your neighbor if you do not first love yourself? Jesus' command clearly indicates that His expectation is for you to love yourself. This doesn't mean you will love everything about yourself. We are all a work in progress. However, to devalue one's own personhood is to insult the God who created you. The psalmist declares that we are "fearfully and wonderfully made" (Psalm 139:14). God has fashioned you with a uniqueness like no other human being. Therefore, we need to accept that uniqueness and choose to take care of ourselves in a way that pleases the Father.

This may be especially difficult for those who grew up in a home or church environment that emphasized sin over the grace and mercy of God. It is true that human beings have an innate inclination to sin. That is why we need a savior, Jesus Christ. However, Jesus never intends for us to wallow in our propensity to sin by using our inner dialogue to berate ourselves for past failures or current struggles. Jesus Christ, the Son of God, came to set us free from all that by imparting His free gift of grace to those who will receive the gift.

Once the gift of grace is imparted to us, we are free to give grace to others, but only after we have been gracious to ourselves. Someone has said that "sometimes the most spiritual thing you can do is take a nap."[25] This addresses one way to address question four in the acrostic. While on earth, Jesus would often withdraw to a solitary place to renew His relationship with His Father. He knew the importance of taking time to be with His Father and rest so He would be at His best, humanly speaking to minister to others. If the sinless Son of God needed to do this on a regular basis, then it makes sense for us to follow His example, so we bring our "A-game" to our daily endeavors.

What action step do you need to take today? Are you hungry? Then, find healthy foods and enjoy consuming those to renew your energy. Are you angry? Then, find a confidante with whom you can share your frustrations, so these frustrations do not spill out inappropriately and negatively impact other people. Are you lonely? Then, flee to your loving Heavenly Father who is a "friend that sticks closer than a brother," or spend quality time with your spouse. The best-case scenario would be to do both! Are you tired? You may need to take a ten-minute break, just to be alone and decompress. Whatever your current need, do not delay in addressing it. You will not regret it, and the people you love will be blessed by your presence. Take care!

---

[25] Alex McFarland, "Sometimes the most spiritual thing you can do is take a nap," The Christian Post, accessed November 28, 2019, https://www.christianpost.com/voice/sometimes-the-most-spiritual-thing-you-can-do-is-take-a-nap.html.

THINK ABOUT IT!

When is the last time you spent time in solitude and silence? Perhaps it has been a while, perhaps you have never tried it, or maybe you are a pro at it. Whatever the case, meditation is worth serious consideration. One definition of meditate is "to focus one's mind for a period of time, in silence or with the aid of chanting, for religious or spiritual purposes or as a method of relaxation."[26]

With the noise and busyness in our daily lives, we could certainly use meditation to restore a sense of calmness, purpose, and vitality. The technological age has certainly brought about many wonderful methods of communication. Cell phones, email, the internet, Facebook, Twitter, Instagram, iPhones, etc., have made instant messaging the norm. However, for all the advantages these bring, there are certainly disadvantages. One disadvantage is clutter. Instant access to communication and information sometimes leads to a cluttered mind that leads one to have a lack of focus at minimum and high stress at maximum. Meditation is one excellent way to restore your equilibrium.

There are various approaches to meditation. One approach is to immerse yourself in nature. There is some-

---

[26] "Meditate," Lexico, powered by Oxford, accessed November 28, 2019, https://www.lexico.com/en/definition/meditate.

thing refreshing about standing outside on a beautiful sunny day and listening to birds sing. Perhaps you are not a bird fan. Then, looking into a flowing stream and listening to the trickling water for a few moments can be a delight. Sometimes these moments of meditation can catch you by surprise, such as when you are driving home from a day of work, and you suddenly notice a beautiful sunset displayed in all its colorful arrays. Even feeling the wind blowing against your face can be a great reminder of nature's God, who allows us to enjoy the world He created.

Another approach to meditation is to look into Scripture, God's Word. Now, meditation should not be confused with Bible reading or Bible study. These certainly have their place, but meditation means focusing intently on one verse or even one phrase. As one focuses on a verse or phrase of Scripture, the truth of the passage becomes a part of you. As food is to the body, God's Word is to the soul. As you slowly meditate, the spiritual digestion begins to take place. With time and consistency, meditation brings about spiritual strength as the power of the Holy Spirit works.

As you can see, the object of meditation is not to empty your mind completely. The object is to put your mind in a position to fill it with the beauty and truth that God provides. Meditation lifts us out of the mundane and trivial and allows us to experience life-giving moments. We have a choice in where to focus our thoughts. We certainly cannot control what happens to us. Often, circumstances are beyond our control. However, you can certainly control the response to those circumstances. You can also choose to build time into your busy schedule to meditate, even if it is for short periods of time.

Jesus alluded to meditation when He commanded us not to worry. In fact, he offered meditation as one way to deal with the worries and cares of this life. Jesus told His followers to "consider the ravens" (Luke 12:24), as an antidote to worrying about what they were going to eat. He also said that we should "consider the lilies" (Matt. 6:28) when worrying about what we are going to wear. Now, Jesus is not telling us we should merely think about ravens and lilies with a passing thought. In the original Greek that recorded His words, the word *consider* means "to think from up to down to a conclusion."[27] This could be thought of in the same way a scientist observes something in order to glean understanding or discover something previously unseen. To *consider* or meditate is to drink deeply of truth or to exercise the mind.

It is important to exercise the mind. You know that bodily exercise is important to overall health, but perhaps, you do not sense or practice the importance of mental exercise. Meditation is one excellent exercise for the mind and spirit. Obviously, the more we exercise the mind, the stronger it will become. The mind should be thought of as an organ that needs development and strengthening. The fact is, your mood, outlook, and approach to life is, in great part, determined by what you feed your mind. When you feed your mind on uncertainties, what is wrong with the world, your own flaws, the flaws of other people, the

---

[27] "Strong's Exhaustive Concordance," Biblehub.com, accessed November 29, 2019 https://biblehub.com/greek/2657.htm.

result will be anxiety and distraction from what is truly important and life giving. Conversely, when you feed your mind on the truths and promises of God's Word, His creation, and the more noble matters of life, you find yourself more focused and better able to enjoy life and bless the lives of others. However, it does take conscious effort and exercise on our part to develop the discipline of meditation that leads to this kind of focus. Perhaps no one puts it better than the apostle Paul who wrote "Whatever is true, whatever is honorable, whatever is right, whatever is pure, whatever is lovely, whatever is good repute, if there is any excellence and if anything worthy of praise, dwell on these things" (Phil. 4:8). And he adds, "And the God of peace will be with you" (Phil. 4:9). Amen!

WHAT'S IN A NAME?

Martin Luther, George Washington, Thomas Jefferson, Abraham Lincoln, Millard Fillmore, Henry Ford, Adolf Hitler, Joseph Stalin, Martin Luther King Jr., Ronald Reagan—just hearing a name brings certain connotations and images to mind. Some of the names in the above list bring thoughts of honor, decency, and leadership. Other names in the list might bring thoughts of obscurity, or even horror, to your mind. There is definitely something in a name!

However, a name simply represents the character and deeds of the individual who possesses it. Let's take the name Adolf. For most of us what comes to mind when we hear the name Adolf are thoughts of atrocities and horror because of what Adolf Hitler did to millions of innocent people. However, had this same man been a benevolent leader, who tried to lift people up instead of exterminating them, quite different images would fill our minds when we hear that name. Obviously, though, the damage has been done and the horrific events associated with his name cannot be erased from our memories.

Did you realize that you, too, are making a name for yourself? As people observe your life, they see the patterns of behavior, positive or negative, that you display on a daily basis. The people closest to you, your family, observe this most closely, and others within your concentric circles of influences observe as well. This is not rocket science. If you treat people with kindness, you will be known as a person of kindness. If, on the other hand, you treat people with a condescending attitude, this becomes evident as well. If you keep your word, your name becomes associated with a person who can be trusted, and if you do not keep your word, the opposite is true as well.

Please do not misunderstand me here. We are not advocating a lifestyle of incessant people pleasing, where a person attempts to appease everyone within the sphere of influence. This is an impossible task! However, the truth is it *is* important what comes to other people's minds when they hear your name mentioned. The author of Proverbs put it this way "A good name is to be more desired than great wealth, Favor is better than silver and gold" (Prov. 22:1). A *good* name is preferable to the wealth of this world. Do you fully realize what this Proverb is conveying? It says that having a good name is far more important than amassing heaps of wealth for someone else to inherit when you are gone. Your good name is of much greater importance than your net worth!

Thus, I have a question. How are you investing in your name? You read that correctly. I didn't ask how you were investing in your retirement portfolio, although I hope you are. It is a smart thing to do, but investing in other people and treating them well is a much greater priority. How do you treat people on a daily basis? We all have our bad days when we slip up. I'm not talking about the occasional blunder. The question refers more to the consistent pattern that is evident in your life and mine. Are you a person who makes a positive contribution to the lives of others?

You may answer by saying, "Well, I may not be making positive contributions, but at least, I'm not making negative contributions either." Really? Do you really want your name to be associated with someone who attempts to add no value to the life of other people? I didn't think so. You desire to be like E. F. Hutton.

You may recall the old commercial, and if you do not, you can google it to see it. The commercials of the 1970s and 1980s had the famous line at the conclusion of each commercial for this stockbroker, "When EF Hutton talks, people listen."[28] This company's point was there really was something to the name because their firm delivered results, and you should believe in their product because of that. When a person has a good track record, it is easy to believe in that person and what they are "selling," so to speak. You may have also discovered that later E. F. Hutton was caught up in a scandal and had to sell the company. Needless to say, the value of their name declined.

What kind of track record do you have? If it is a good one, then keep investing in people and maintain that "good name." If it is not a good track record, please understand a wonderfully redeeming truth. No one's track record is irredeemable. By the grace of God, you can do what is necessary to repair that track record and begin a journey

---

[28] "When E.F. Hutton Talks People Listen, vintage TV commercial," You Tube, accessed November 29, 2019, https://www.youtube.com/watch?v=2MXqb1a3Apg.

where you restore people's trust by the consistent manner in which you add value to their lives. Whatever situation you find yourself in, always remember that a good name is worth the investment.

THINGS I LEARNED FROM MY MOM

Back in 1987, country singers Glen Campbell and Steve Wariner released the song "The Hand that Rocks the Cradle."[29] There is much truth contained in the words of this song. Our mothers should be honored and celebrated for their positive influence in our lives. Long after they depart from this earth, they continue to influence their sons and daughters. Moms truly have an eternal impact on their children. I acknowledge that not all moms are positive influences, and that some actually exert negative influences in the lives of their children. And for most, there is a mix of positive and negative habits from which to glean. For the purposes of this writing, I want to focus on some of the positive truths I learned from my mom.

From the earliest time in my life, I remember my mom singing to me as a child. As she held me close and rocked me, she would sing, "Jesus loves the little children, all the children of the world, Red and yellow, black, and white they are precious in His sight. Jesus loves the little children of the world."[30]

---

[29] Campbell, Glen and Steve Wariner, 1987, "The Hand That Rocks the Cradle," May 30, 1987, *Still Within the Sound of My Voice*, album.
[30] Woolston, C. Herbert and George F. Root, Public Domain.

The melody of songs has a tendency to stick with us. Thus, having a mom who sings to her children is a double blessing. There is the blessing of hearing her voice, and then the blessing of having the words teach the child. With this particular song, I learned a couple of things. First, that Jesus loves all children, regardless of ethnicity. The song acknowledges there are differences in people, but those differences do not matter to Jesus. Jesus loves people the way His Father created them.

Second, if Jesus loves all children, and I am a child, that means Jesus loves me. Early in life, I knew Jesus loved me because of a mom who sang that truth to me. This led me to have regard for other people. Occasionally, I would hear someone make a derogatory comment about someone with a different ethnicity. I knew this did not line up with truth. I did not know this because I was especially endowed with some kind of supernatural knowledge. I knew this because I had a mother who taught it to me through her singing that little chorus to me. The songs that moms sing to their children, or allow their children to hear, influences their worldview! Now, that's leadership!

How many have often recited the well-known words of this prayer before a meal? "God is great. God is good. Let us thank Him for our food. By His hands we are fed. Give us, Lord, our daily bread. Amen." My mom would often lead us in this prayer before eating a meal she had prepared. I learned multiple truths from this. First, God is great. There is no one like God. He is big. He is mighty and He is strong. Second, He is good. God's nature is one of goodness. He is not some cosmic force just waiting to zap you if you mess up. His nature is one of kindness toward His creation. Third, I learned that it is appropriate to express thanks to God from whom all blessings flow. He is the provider of our daily needs. Finally, I learned to ask God for what I need, not what I want. Daily bread is an obvious necessity. It is appropriate to ask for daily bread, and not a Lamborghini!

Whether it be the brief chorus of a song or a brief prayer, moms impact the thinking of their children. As one can see from the previous examples, it doesn't have to be an elaborate lecture or ritual to influence. I am sure you have already noticed that these first examples were both poems. This makes a case for using poetry and songs to positively influence the next generation. The rhyme and rhythm of language is something the human brain responds to. We need to use it for good and not for evil. There are plenty of rhymes and rhythms in society that are used as negative influences. I am grateful for a mom who, even though she may not have realized it, used these tools to influence my worldview in a good way.

Mom also influenced me with quotes during her lifetime. One quote she often made was the idiom "pretty is as pretty does." This little idiom is packed with truth. She was teaching her son that there are many pretty faces out there, but that a pretty face doesn't necessarily mean pretty behavior. She was teaching me that behavior is of greater importance than one's physical appearance. We live in a society obsessed with physical appearances. It was true when I was a kid, and it's even more true now. Mom knew that, and she gave me the gift of truth with this oft-repeated phrase.

Another oft-repeated phrase Mom used was "A wise man changes his mind, but a fool never will." I didn't like hearing her say this as a child because I saw someone changing his mind about something as weakness. I was of the mind-set that someone should stake out an opinion on something and stick to it. However, I didn't understand until years later what she was teaching me. She was trying to teach me that a wise person will listen to another person's point of view and that sometimes that wise person will change his/her point of view based on new information or a line of thinking not previously considered. It's true that the Bible has the final word on everything. However, when it comes to opinions on matters of no eternal significance, one's opinion should be open to the consideration of the opinion of others as well. There is nothing more unappealing than a person who thinks he/she is right about everything.

Mom taught me with more than tunes or quotes. She taught me through actions as well. Mom was a giver, not a taker. She delighted in giving gifts to others, whether it was a specially baked food or a birthday gift. Giving was her love language, and she did it almost to a fault. Mom grew up during the Great Depression of the 1930s and 1940s in the United States. She said it was a good Christmas when they received fresh fruit in their stocking! Therefore, Mom wanted to make sure her children and others whom she loved got to experience more exciting Christmases and birthdays than she did. Mom had a way of making one feel special. Moms are good that way. Many young people in today's twenty-first century could use "surrogate moms" to fill in the "feeling special" gap.

Even during my mom's last months on this earth, she was thinking of others. As she lay in a health care facility, completely dependent on others for her well-being, she would often refer to others who in her mind were in worse shape than she and how she would pray for them often. Even in her suffering, she was putting other people's needs before her own. Society could use more people like this!

Yes, there "ought to be a hall of fame for mamas,"[31] but as long as people have mamas like mine, the memories of those mamas will be enshrined in the minds of their children, and the legacy they leave behind will continue to have impact for generations to come. It is better to be enshrined in the memories of those you love than to be in a thousand hall of fames enshrined for those who do not know you.

---

[31] Campbell, Glen and Steve Wariner, 1987, "The Hand That Rocks the Cradle," May 30, 1987, *Still Within the Sound of My Voice*, album.

THE BEST PARENTING: MODELING

It was Michigan's poet laureate, Edgar Guest, who wrote many years ago, "I'd rather see a sermon than hear one any day; I'd rather one should walk with me than merely tell the way, The eye's a better pupil and more willing than the ear, Fine counsel is confusing, but example's always clear."[32] This is true for all of life, and especially true in parenting. At some point, children turn a deaf ear to the lecture of the parent. It's true that boundaries must be set and enforced. It is also true that the motto "Do as I say and not as I do" is ludicrous. Children rarely rise above the example of the parent. Sure, there are exceptions to this statement. However, generally speaking, it is the parent's modeling of the right values and habits that will carry the day in the child's life and into their future.

I was only a few months old when my father decided to kick the smoking habit. As he held me in his arms, I would naturally reach into his shirt pocket and pull out a cigarette. My dad did not decide to kick the smoking habit because it made him feel bad. To the contrary, he enjoyed smoking. He decided to kick the smoking habit because he

---

[32] Guest, Edgar A., "Sermons We See," Public Domain.

knew that if he continued, that little boy he was holding in his arms would most likely pick up the habit and suffer from all the ill health effects involved. Dad kicked the habit for the sake of his son, and I am grateful.

I'm wondering how many other habits need to be broken for the sake of a son or daughter. Someone has said, "What adults do in moderation, children will do in excess." Children internalize the behaviors they see displayed in their parents. The influence of a parent on a child is astronomical. Every little boy wants to be like his father, and every little girl adores her mother. It does not take very long for one to observe that children begin to quickly emulate the behaviors of the parent. After all, the parent is the first and most important teacher of the child.

This parent modeling of behavior works in positive and negative ways. First, let's take the positive. If you want your child to be kind to others, then let your child see and hear you being kind to others. If you want your child to love God, then love God yourself. If you want your child to become a person of prayer, then let your child see and hear you pray. This could carry over into just about any area of life. If you want your child to grow up one day and be a loving spouse, then you must be a loving spouse as well. If you want your child to give grace to people, instead of incessantly criticizing them, then be sure that you are a grace dispenser to others and to your children too.

It takes many years for a child to unlearn the behavior patterns of a parent, both good and bad. If you use bad language, your child will most likely use bad language, and we have to monitor other influences like television and internet as well. One of my own sons was about four years old when he heard the sounds of a commercial truck in the neighborhood making the loud beeping sound those trucks make when put in reverse. When he heard these startling sounds, he uttered the words, "What the hell!" Now, my wife and I are not saints. However, we did not use those words, especially around the children. Where had he picked that up? From a movie that he watched, and a classic western at that! Now, it is impossible to eliminate all hints of bad language, bad attitudes, and bad habits from our children's lives. However, even a slight amount of exposure to something unsavory or inappropriate can influence our children. The good example our children see in us must outweigh the bad examples they see on television, the internet, and in society.

Sometimes, we must eliminate what seem to be harmless habits for the sake of our children. When I was in my early twenties, I would occasionally smoke a cigar. My reasoning went something like this, "A cigar is not as bad for you as a cigarette because you just puff on a cigar instead of inhaling like a cigarette." Even today, many years later, I occasionally get the urge to puff on a cigar, but I refrain from doing that. Why? I refrain for the sake of my sons. I do not want them to get started on a habit that will be difficult for them to stop and experience the potential health issues that come with it. You may say, "Smoking an occasional cigar is harmless. You are being far too strict on yourself and your sons." Even if true, I would rather err on the side of caution. Far too many people today are addicted to substances, thought patterns, and images because of a first try or first glance. We must discipline our lives for the sake of our children.

None of these truths are original with me. The very One who embodies truth, Jesus Christ, modeled truth for His first followers. For example, He didn't just tell them to serve others. Toward the end of His earthly ministry, He did the unthinkable when he took a water basin and a towel and began to wash His disciples' feet. This task was reserved for the lowest and least in that society. Yet He chose to do the dirtiest of tasks to demonstrate how he wanted His disciples to serve others. They could do this because they saw their Master and Teacher model this for them.

The same is true for parenting. We must exemplify the behaviors and attitudes we want to see in our children. We will not be perfect models. However, we must try to be the best models possible, as the grace of God enables us. By His grace, He will multiply the effects to benefit our children. We can and we must. Our children are worth it!

LEADERSHIP: IT'S ABOUT PASSION, JUDGMENT, COMMUNICATION, AND INTEGRITY

Leadership boils down to four things: integrity, passion, judgment, and communication. Perhaps this is making a complex subject and endeavor too simple. However, if you don't have these fabulous four, you don't have leadership.

Let's begin with integrity. One meaning of the word *integrity* is "the quality or state of being complete or undivided."[33] A leader must be a person whose beliefs, convictions, words, and actions match. This doesn't mean that the leader will be one without mistakes. In fact, sometimes, the leader will act in ways that do not align with his/her beliefs. However, the great leader is quick to acknowledge this and offer apologies, thereby, keeping integrity intact. Outside of the occasional snafu, the effective leader has a *pattern* of integrity. One does not have to wonder what the effective leader believes or deems important. It is evident in the daily life and decisions of the leader as the pattern is set.

---

[33] "Integrity," Merriam-Webster Dictionary, accessed December 2, 2019, https://www.merriam-webster.com/dictionary/integrity.

The apostle Paul knew something about setting a pattern. He wrote to the church at Corinth and told them "Be imitators of me, just as I also am of Christ" (1 Cor. 11:1). Paul was not claiming to be flawless. However, he disciplined himself (see 1 Cor. 9:27) to the point that he could confidently call on the people he loved to follow his example and any effective leader will do the same today. Great leaders have a clearly defined set of beliefs and convictions and daily monitor their words and actions to ensure integrity. Without integrity, followers lose confidence in a leader, and when follower confidence is lost, all is lost.

This brings us to the force behind and within every great leader—passion. The dictionary definition of passion is "strong and barely controllable emotion."[34] It is that force from within that propels the leader forward. The effective leader is passionate about beliefs, the organization, and the mission to be accomplished by the company or organization. Passion is what enables the effective leader to continue, even when obstacles are encountered. And obstacles will be encountered. They are inevitable. There will always be those who do not believe in the mission of an organization or those within the organization who may believe in the mission, but not with the same passion of the leader. Therefore, the leader must be *the* most passionate person in the organization. Spiritually speaking, passion is strong desire given and controlled by God.

---

[34] "Passion," Oxford Reference, accessed December 2, 2019, https://www.oxfordreference.com/view/10.1093/acref/9780198609810.001.0001/acref-9780198609810-e-5266.

We turn once again to the writing of the apostle Paul who writes "For it is God who is at work in you, both to will and to work for His good pleasure" (Phil. 2:13). God uses people to accomplish His purposes. He also equips people with what they need to do this. When you act because of God-given passion, little will deter you from fulfilling your God-given mission. We are not speaking just about church leaders or missionaries. Certainly, these are included. However, when referring to leadership, we are referencing any field such as business, education, law, medicine, science, law enforcement, the arts, etc. God is at work in people of all professions and has purposes to accomplish in these fields. In spite of the evil present in the world, God loves people and wants to redeem them for His purposes. A passionate leader will lead with this in mind and function as one led by God and God's heart for people.

Leadership is a series of decision-making and using good judgment. A leader must daily make one decision after another, and sometimes, in rapid fashion. This is why it's important to have the above two characteristics in place first, for if they are not in place, it certainly complicates the decision-making process, and leaders make decisions with no strong anchor or compass in place. Making decisions without a strong anchor or compass leads to inconsistent decisions on the part of the leader and breeds distrust and misunderstanding among followers.

Leaders must be able to deliberate and come to what the dictionary calls "considered decisions or sensible conclusions" or judgment.[35] However, the leader must take the

---

[35] "Judgement," Lexico, accessed December 2, 2019, https://www.lexico.com/en/definition/judgement.

right amount of time to review options. A snap decision with little consideration could lead to a bad decision. Abraham Lincoln had a Union general during the Civil War, General George McClellan, who was a great planner, but who failed to execute his plans, which led to Lincoln commenting that McClellan had "the slows."[36] Being paralyzed by indecisiveness is something an effective leader needs to avoid.

Finally, without the ability to communicate one's decisions and expectations, a leader will be ineffective. A leader can have the best ideas and strategies imaginable, but without the ability to effectively communicate these and get others to buy into them, these ideas and strategies will not come to fruition. An effective leader must remember the three *Cs* of communication—clarity, conciseness, and consistency. A leader must remember that just because something has been communicated does not mean it has been understood. Each person has a way of interpreting a message through his/her unique filter. Therefore, the effective leader anticipates this and seeks to communicate clearly with details and illustrations to minimize misunderstanding. There will always be those who misinterpret, but the effective leader communicates with this in mind and presents with clarity on the front end. The origin of word clarity is Middle English, where it meant "glory or divine splendor,"[37] and indeed, it seems divine when a message goes out to others and is genuinely understood!

---

[36] "He Still Has the Slows," Forbes, accessed December 2, 2019, https://www.forbes.com/forbes/2009/0413/013-bernanke-fed-credit-still-has-slows.html#18035d3b7f55.

[37] "Clarity," Lexico, accessed December 2, 2019, https://www.lexico.com/en/definition/clarity.

Secondly, communication must be concise. The dictionary defines concise as "brief in form, but comprehensive in scope."[38] To be brief and comprehensive at the same time can be quite a challenge. However, the effective leader gives just enough detail to be clear. Failure to communicate in this manner can result in becoming convoluted in the presence of too much verbiage. Furthermore, in today's fast-paced information-packed world, people are prone to missing the point if one belabors it too long.

Finally, a leader's message must be consistent. To be effective, a leader must communicate the same message over and over again. The emphasis here is on two ideas. First, an effective leader ensures that the message delivered today is the same message delivered yesterday. Failure to do this leads to followers musing about a leader with a forked tongue. Although a leader might use different illustrations for the same message in order to effectively convey the message, the message must remain the same. Secondly, the effective leader realizes that repetition is necessary as some may not have "gotten the message" the first time. Repetition is both an effective learning and communication strategy. The effective leader keeps the message before the people to ensure the people are following.

One may ask, what if communication fails? What if I do all of the above, and people still do not get it? The answer, though perhaps simplistic, is you listen. Listening is a vital part of communication that cannot be ignored. Often, people simply want to convey their concerns and

---

[38] "Concise," Dictionary.com, accessed December 2, 2019, https://www.dictionary.com/browse/concise.

know they have been heard. Listening also gives insight into the follower's fears and misunderstandings and allows the leader to quell their fears and clarify misunderstanding to ensure that all are on the same page.

Though having integrity, passion, judgment, and communication does not guarantee that everyone will follow, these four characteristics provide a solid foundation for leadership. And you know what happens when one does not have a solid foundation. Build your leadership on these four qualities, and you are off to a great start in positively influencing others to be on mission with you.

I'M SORRY

Perhaps this is the most underutilized phrase in the English language. Why? Because in order to use it, we must put ourselves in a position of humility and admit that a wrong has been committed. As humans, we do not like to admit we were wrong about something, whether it's an opinion wrongly held, a word wrongly uttered, or a deed done to another person that brought injury. Telling someone we are sorry about something puts us at the mercy of another person. And human beings do not like to be at the mercy of another. However, we would find that the world would be a much better place in which to live if we uttered this phrase more often.

In order to realize that the phrase needs to be uttered in a relationship, at least a couple of things need to be true of us. First, we must be sensitive to the needs and feelings of another person. We cannot have an "it's all about me attitude" and also consider other people's feelings. Second, we have to be introspective enough to evaluate our own actions to determine what type of impact our actions have on other people. These two seem diametrically opposed to one another. However, both must be true for us to consider other people.

The sentiment of much of society is that the phrase "I'm sorry" is an unnecessary phrase to use. We are influenced by the spirit of the age and modern pop culture here. Perhaps you have heard the phrase "Love means never having to say you're sorry."[39] It is derived from Erich Segal's novel *Love Story* and said twice in the 1970s film adaptation.

This phrase implies that if one genuinely loves a person enough, the other person in the relationship never needs to admit a mistake or make right a careless word said or careless deed done. This is utter nonsense! As fallible human beings, each of us fail to treat others, at times, in the manner they deserve to be treated. We do not always have an "I'll do what is best for others" mentality. When we fail to have that mentality, we inevitably treat others in a manner that is inappropriate. When those occasions occur, the best action to take is to humble oneself before the other person and admit the mistake and utter the often-underused phrase "I'm sorry."

I am reminded of the 1970s character Fonzie, in the popular show *Happy Days*.[40] The Fonz had an overly healthy opinion of himself. He was suave, cool, popular with girls and feared by the guys. If you remember the show, he had almost supernatural-like powers in a comedic way. However, this character had at least one flaw, and that is he could not even utter the words "I'm sorry." This provided for some funny moments in the show and amusement for those watching. However, there is nothing amusing in real life about someone who is unwilling or unable to say these words.

In order to be able to use these words, we must be able to feel regret. Regret is that feeling brought about by the

---

[39] Segal, Erich, 1970, *Love Story*.
[40] Marshall, Garry, 1974–1984, *Happy Days*.

realization that we have brought harm or injury to another person, even if it is simply an emotional or mental harm. Regret is not often seen in the best light. If people dwell too long on what could have been or what should have been, life will be lived, looking backwards and will become dismal for the one with that outlook. However, regret can be a good thing when we realize we have harmed another person. When felt in this sense, regret can and should lead to an acknowledgement of wrong doing and a plea of "I'm sorry" to the person harmed.

Society has been bombarded with the sentiment "I should feel good about myself." The modern self-esteem movement implies that even a twinge of regret is not a good thing. We must feel good about ourselves at all costs. However, this sentiment is harmful and leads to relationships that are self-indulgent. Perhaps this is one reason divorce is so common in our day. One cannot be married for too long to a self-indulgent person and expect to have a successful marriage. A successful marriage takes two people who are willing to sacrifice their own needs for the other person's needs and two people who are willing to say "I'm sorry."

Popular culture has not been helpful in this area either. If we believe what we see in movies about marriage, we set unrealistic expectations for our spouse. Many of the relationships we see in film are characterized by romantic notions that do not play themselves out in the day-to-day life of marriage and the family. There should be romance in a marriage, and it is unhealthy when the romance leaves a marriage. However, there is so much more to marriage than the romantic aspect. There is sacrifice, and there is the admitting of wrongdoing and restoration that must often take place.

It is also imperative to follow up the "I'm sorry" phrase with yet another phrase. I am referring to the phrase, "Will you forgive me?" You see, it's not enough to admit wrongdoing. We must seek the release and restoration that forgiveness provides. When we receive forgiveness from the person we have wronged, it brings a releasing of debt from that person that says, "You no longer owe me" and "I have absolved your debt." This begins to bring healing and wholeness to the relationship. This is true in a marriage, a church, a workplace, or friendship. It is true that the "I'm sorry" mentality can be used excessively. However, the likelihood is that in most relationships, this humble mentality is not used frequently enough. From whom do you need to seek forgiveness today? It begins with two words. Go ahead. It will make things better.

Jesus said in Matthew 6:14–15 "For if you forgive others for their transgressions, your heavenly Father will also forgive you. But if you do not forgive others, then your Father will not forgive your transgressions."

MASLOW WAS PARTIALLY CORRECT

If you have done even a cursory reading of psychology theories, no doubt you have come across Abraham Maslow's hierarchy of needs.[41] Maslow's theory concerning human motivation came out in the 1940s and 1950s and has been required reading in many fields of study, including education. Maslow says that human need is based on an ascending hierarchy of needs, beginning with physiological needs and climbing all the way to self-actualization. He believed that one level of need had to be met first before the next level could be met.

In other words, a person's basic human need of food, shelter, and clothing must be met before a person's safety needs could be met. After all, if a person is hungry all the time, how can they be concerned about meeting any other needs if the basic need of hunger is not met first. For good reasons teachers have used this theory for decades, realizing that a hungry child will not be apt to learn at high levels if the basic need for food is not met first. The United States government recognizes this, as well, providing a hot break-

---

[41] "Maslow's Hierarchy of Needs," Simply Psychology, accessed December 2, 2019, https://www.simplypsychology.org/maslow.html.

fast and hot lunch for students in public schools throughout the country and free/reduced meals for those families who live in poverty. This is where Maslow's hierarchy makes sense.

Furthermore, if a person does not feel safe, how can the person even begin to have his/her love and belonging needs met? If a person feels unsafe, it is highly unlikely that the person will feel loved. The implications of this truth have many ramifications for our society and the neighborhoods in which many of our nation's families live. I'm not sure we even can begin to know the impact that living in an unsafe environment and feeling the threat that comes with it has on the individuals who live in such environments. For example, a battered wife cannot have her love/belonging needs met living under the glare and threat of a husband who may go off at any moment, neither can a child have love/belonging needs met under the oppression of an angry or violent parent.

Thus, climbing the hierarchy, it makes sense that a person who has basic physiological needs met, lives in a safe environment, and has love/belonging through meaningful relationships with others will then have the esteem that one needs. However, this is not always the case. There are people who appear to have all the aforementioned in place yet do not esteem themselves very highly.

What is at the heart of this issue? Is it a chemical imbalance? Maybe. I am not a doctor and am not qualified to make that judgment. I understand that biological issues can certainly impact people in very real and, sometimes, painful ways. Thus, I am not minimizing this possibility.

However, aside from a medical issue, how is it that people who have what Maslow would refer to as physiological, safety, and love/belonging needs met, still persist in devaluing themselves and possibly others?

I believe that for many this inability stems from too much focus on self. At the top of Maslow's hierarchy is *self*-actualization. For Maslow, this was the ultimate goal. If everything below this pinnacle lined up, then one could fulfill his/her potential and reach untold levels of fulfillment and success. However, I believe Maslow's theory is flawed at this point. An excessive focus on self is a humanistic view of life, and self-fulfillment or actualization is not the ultimate goal of life. We do not have to look very far to see those who seem to have the best of what life has to offer, and yet do not live fulfilling lives, evidenced by moving from one relationship to another, remaining in an abusive relationship, becoming addicted to a substance, and ultimately, taking one's own life or that of another. No, a focus on self leads to fulfilling one's desires at all costs, without regarding another. This never ends very well.

Jesus Christ put it this way "For whoever wishes to save his life will lose it; but whoever loses his life for My sake will find it" (Matt. 16:25). Maslow's focus was fulfilling self. Jesus's focus was in denying self. He said "If any of you wants to be my follower, you must give up your own way, take up your cross, and follow me" (Matt. 16:24). Maslow's focus is from a humanistic world view. Jesus's focus is from a biblical world view. These viewpoints are the polar opposites of one another. The truth Jesus was conveying was that the surrender of self to Him would lead to ultimate fulfillment. It makes sense to allow the one who cocreated the universe and died to redeem mankind to tell us how to have ultimate fulfillment. We don't need self-actualization. We need Christ-actualization. And this happens through a relationship with Him.

The Christ follower seeks to please the One who has redeemed his/her soul from death. It is only by delighting in Christ that we find complete fulfillment. Someone has characterized it this way:

J—Jesus
O—Others
Y—Yourself

As we put Jesus first, then seek to be more interested in meeting the needs of others, and lastly, take care of ourselves, we live life as God intended us to live it and find joy in the journey.

Maslow was close, but he didn't have it completely right. We should take what Maslow was right about and use it to inform our relationships with others and help us as we seek to take care of human needs as Jesus taught in the gospel of Matthew, chapter 25. However, we should realize that we need to refer to the JOY hierarchy—putting Jesus first, others second, and self last—if we are to be fulfilled in life.

THE MAJESTY OF GOD

God reigns over the nations, God sits on His holy throne.
—Psalm 47:8

The Lord reigns, He is clothed with majesty; the Lord has clothed and girded Himself with strength; Indeed, the world is firmly established, it will not be moved. Your throne is established from of old; You are from everlasting.
—Psalm 93:1–2

The Lord has established His throne in the heavens, and His sovereignty rules over all.
—Psalm 103:19

What comes to mind when you think of the word *majesty*? Perhaps the image that comes to mind is that of a regal king in England or Scotland, sitting on his throne with scepter in hand, with subjects who bow before him. Perhaps you are a nature lover, and the splendor of mountains rising to meet the azure blue on a sunny day fills your mind with an example of what the word *majesty* could mean. *Merriam-Webster* defines *majesty* as "sovereign power, authority, or dignity."[42]

---

[42] "Majesty," Merriam-Webster, accessed December 2, 2019, https://www.merriam-webster.com/dictionary/majesty.

It is interesting to see who or what people ascribe majesty to. Oppressive countries led by dictators often have followers that ascribe majesty to them. I was amazed with the reaction of the people of North Korea when their dictator, Kim Jong Il, died in 2011. North Korean citizens appeared in public in huge numbers to openly weep over their leader's death. Even though he was a leader who had kept them in the darkness and cut off from the rest of the world, they thought he was god. People are created to worship, and they will attach themselves to what they perceive as majestic, whether or not the object is worthy of veneration in that way.

We see this in our society as well. Sports figures, political leaders, religious authorities, musical artists, and charismatic personalities are esteemed highly by many to the point of unhealthy adoration. The problem is not in being interested in these individuals, but in having an obsessive interest in them to the point of worship. However, we should not be surprised when this happens. It has been said that Blaise Pascal, a famous French mathematician and philosopher, wrote, "There is a God-shaped vacuum in the heart of every man which cannot be filled by any created thing, but only by God the Creator, made known through Jesus Christ."[43]

Human beings often try to fill the God-shaped vacuum with many things other than God Himself. And perhaps, we can understand why. After all, one cannot see God. Thus, it

---

[43] "Quotable Quote," Goodreads, accessed December 2, 2019, https://www.goodreads.com/quotes/801132-there-is-a-god-shaped-vacuum-in-the-heart-of-each.

becomes difficult for many to believe in what they perceive to be an impersonal, distant force. This is not new. We see this illustrated over and over again in the ancient history of Israel. Moses had not been on the mountain very long before the Israelites crafted a golden calf to worship. They thought they needed a tangible object in which they could pour their adoration. We see this again when all the nations surrounding them had a human king. They wanted to be just like the other nations. No longer were they content with allowing God to govern them. They craved a human leader, and God granted their desire. Thus, the only theocracy that ever existed in human history came to an end.

However, we see in the hymnbook of Israel in Psalm 104:1–2 "Bless the Lord, O my soul! O Lord my God, You are very great; You are clothed with splendor and majesty, Covering Yourself with splendor and majesty, Covering Yourself with light as with a cloak, Stretching out heaven like a tent curtain." We find in these verses a recognition of the power and majesty of God. Though God cannot be seen with the human eye, we can see evidence of who He is as we gaze at the majesty revealed in the heavens that He has "stretched out like a tent curtain." He has given us evidence of His creative ability.

Furthermore, we see evidence of His intimate involvement in the creation of human beings. The psalmist wrote "For You formed my inward parts; You wove me in my mother's womb. I will give thanks to You, for I am fearfully and wonderfully made; Wonderful are Your works, And my soul knows it very well" (Psalm 139:13–14). The miracle of how God has crafted all the human body systems to work together is one that should not go unnoticed. Therefore, whether in the vast expanse of the heavens or the intricate details of the human body, God's majesty is clearly revealed.

It is interesting that even in some Christian circles of worship, the majesty of God is not always clearly seen, especially in the United States. Too often, the focus of song lyrics is about how the worshipper relates to God instead of on who God is in all His attributes. Furthermore, the focus in many churches is on a dynamic, charismatic personality in the form of the senior pastor. What does an unbalanced focus on self in song lyrics indicate about the Christian church? What does an obsessive focus on the personality of the pastor say about us? I would submit that if the focus of songs is more on ourselves than God, then we are worshipping ourselves. Certainly, it is appropriate to sing about what God has done in our lives, but the focus should always be on Him. It is also right to respect pastors who accurately preach the word of God. However, if a person talks more about what the pastor is doing at church instead of what God is doing, there is a potential "cult personality" issue at hand.

It is time for the majesty of God to be restored in churches across the land. When we fail to exalt the majesty and beauty of God as demonstrated through His Son, Jesus Christ, other things capture our hearts and demand to be worshipped. May we exalt the Only One worthy of worship so the "God-shaped vacuum" can be filled with His majesty.

FROM COFFEE TO CHRIST

An old 1980s/1990s coffee commercial claims the best part of waking up is smelling their coffee. It was a nice marketing strategy and came with a catchy jingle that was difficult to get out of your mind. You know, I think they were on to something. Oh, make no mistake, they were trying to sell their coffee, but sometimes, the best thing you can do in the morning is enjoy the aroma and taste of good coffee. After all, it is one of those "little" blessings we often take for granted.

How many other "little" blessings do we take for granted on a daily basis? I have this theory. It goes like this—if people were more grateful, they would be happier. It is hard to be grateful and unhappy at the same time. And sometimes, gratitude for the "little things" is what keeps up going. When the circumstances of life and stress of job and family seem to overwhelm, we can find comfort and encouragement in everyday blessings.

Have you learned to appreciate the value of what your eyes behold and what your ears hear on a daily basis? We can often become unaware of the beauty that is in the world around us. Decades ago, as a younger man, I recall a time in my life when it seemed that all around me was caving in. I was distressed over many things. Then, I will never forget this. All of a sudden, one day as I was exiting my home, and I looked around and realized that the beauty of spring had arrived, and I was struck by the greenness of the trees all around. It had been there for some time, but I just hadn't noticed. You see, my focus was on my circumstances instead of the beauty that existed all around me.

Beauty exists around us everywhere. What beauty are you missing today? Have you noticed the warmth of the sunshine on your face or the beauty of the snowflakes, each one unique, as they fall gently to the earth? Have you delighted in the uninhibited laughter of a child or the wisdom of an older person? Did you notice the beautiful smile of the person who just walked by or the fragrance of their perfume or cologne? Did you allow the firmness of a handshake or the tenderness of a kiss to encourage your spirit as a result of human affection?

Have you gazed at the beauty of a sunset or wondered at the grandeur of a mountain or contemplated as the rhythm of ocean waves pounded the beach? Yes, these are all opportunities for gratitude and appreciation for all the blessings God has given. When the forces of life are daunting, and sometimes they are daunting indeed, we must find ways to appreciate the stability of the blessings God allows us to experience every day.

I have often found comfort by looking into the night sky at the stars and the moon. I can remember enjoying their beauty, even as a young child. Even now, as a middle-aged man, I can gaze at those same stars and moon and know they haven't changed. They are still there doing what they do, and I can rejoice in that. I can rejoice in knowing that although many things in the world have changed in the last fifty years, those majestic lights in the night sky have not changed. These objects are still doing what God created them to do. They are constant, and I take comfort in knowing that no matter how drastically the circumstances of life or the values of society may change, the stars and the moon and the God who created them have not changed.

The Bible says "Jesus Christ is the same yesterday, today, and forever" (Heb. 13:8). The beauty of the character and nature of God is yet another blessing in which we can delight when the going gets tough. The beauty I am referring to is not a physical beauty. We find that Isaiah prophesied about Christ by saying "He has no stately form or majesty that we should look upon Him, nor appearance that we should be attracted to Him" (Isa. 53:2). The beauty that we see demonstrated in Jesus Christ is the love of God the Father in punishing His own Son so that our guilt could be removed. Isaiah goes on to write "The Lord was pleased to crush Him [Jesus the Christ], putting Him to grief if He would render Himself a guilt offering" (Isa. 53:10). And that is what Jesus the Messiah did! It is beauty that One would offer His life for another, so another could live and be forgiven. In a world where the word *sacrifice* is sometimes an unpalatable word, there is beauty in what the Son of Almighty God did on the cross.

Notice the word Isaiah used in the above verse. He writes that God was "pleased." How could the God of the universe be pleased to crush His one and only Son? The answer is that it pleased Him because this was the way for you and me to receive forgiveness and come into a relationship with Him. God was pleased to do this because He loves you! This is amazing beauty. Have you experienced the beauty of God manifested through His Son, Jesus the Christ? If not, you can. And if you have experienced His beauty, are your delighting in His beauty on a daily basis? This is One constant that we have in spite of the shifting sands of time.

So what are you waiting on? Wake up and smell the coffee. Enjoy its taste as you face the new day God has made. Then, look into God's Word, the Bible, and experience the beauty of His love and His truth for you. It's going to be a beautiful day!

DON'T DISPUTE MY WORD

I got in trouble many times as a boy for doing things I should not be doing. Embarrassingly, I would sometimes argue with my father when he was counseling me in a discipline situation. My father would often say to me during my plea, "Don't dispute my word." In other words, he was saying to me, "My word is final. End of story. This is the way it is." As I reflect on those days, I think he was also trying to convey something of even greater importance to me. My father knew that if I would dispute his word, I would more likely dispute the ultimate Word, the Word from the Heavenly Father.

The world suffers from a tremendous crisis today, a crisis of *disputing God's Word*, the Bible. Many people see the Bible as nothing more than a book of literature. Some may even believe it is a *great* work of literature or history. However, many of those same people would maintain that the Bible is not God's Word. They would claim it is not God's revelation of Himself to humanity. Some see it as a book that has no relevance in today's sophisticated society and certainly no principles by which people's lives should be lived.

How did American society arrive at such a conclusion? Some would say it occurred during the 1960s, the age of liberation, when sexual mores changed, and people began to flaunt individual choice and fulfillment as supreme.

Others would point to the 1962 Supreme Court decision that made staff-led prayer illegal in public schools. Of course, we know that as long as exams are given in public schools, there will always be prayer.

Others might say society got off course with the evolution debate of the 1920s and the famous Scopes Monkey Trial of 1925. Of course, Darwin's theories began to be published in the late 1850s, and his theories were taught in universities for decades before the Scopes trial. Some would contend that society began to go astray when higher criticism began to be taught in universities and seminaries. They would say that higher criticism led to people questioning the authority and inspiration of God's Word, as it began to find flaws with the transmission of Scripture and supposed inaccuracies in its recording.

Some believe we got off course during the Age of Enlightenment of the seventeenth and eighteenth centuries, in which reason and science was exalted as supreme. The movement spanned an ocean crossing Europe into the United States, following the American Revolution. Others would say that things went amiss when Ivy League universities, the oldest in the country, began to change course and leave the purposes for which they were founded as leading seminaries for the training of ministers. It *is* interesting to note that Harvard's rules and precepts as adopted in 1636 stated (original spelling),

> Let every Student be plainly instructed, and earnestly pressed to consider well, the maine end of his life and

> studies is, to know God and Jesus Christ which is eternal life (John 17:3) and therefore to lay Christ in the bottome, as the only foundation of all sound knowledge and Learning. And seeing the Lord only giveth wisdome, Let every one seriously set himself by prayer in secret to seeke it of him (Prov. 2:3).
>
> Every one shall so exercise himselfe in reading the Scriptures twice a day, that he shall be ready to give such an account of his proficiency therein, both in Theoreticall observations of Language and Logick, and in practical and spiritual truths, as his Tutor shall require, according to his ability; seeing the entrance of the word giveth light, it giveth understanding to the simple (Psalm 119:130).[44]

Some would say Americans have strayed from our moorings over the centuries because the priesthood had a monopoly on interpreting God's Word, and the pronouncements of a church, in many cases, took priority over the authority of God's Word. While all of the above may have certainly had an impact on where we are today, the problem with questioning God's Word began long before any of these events.

---

[44] "Shield and 'Veritas' History," Harvard GSAS Christian Community, accessed December 2, 2019, http://www.hcs.harvard.edu/~gsascf/shield-and-veritas-history/.

The questioning of God's Word began shortly after the beginning of time in the Garden of Eden, when the crafty serpent asked "Did God really say?" (Gen. 3:1). Those four words began a cataclysmic movement that has spiraled out of control throughout the centuries. Adam and Eve bought into the crafty serpent's approach. Oh, the serpent went on to spout lies about how Adam and Eve would be enlightened once they partook of the forbidden fruit. However, it all began with questioning what God had told them. This is where all sin begins. As humans, we often believe God is holding out on us. We believe that He is keeping us from what is in our best interest, and we begin to question Him. And when we do, we set ourselves up for the lie that the enemy is ready to feed us and matters go downhill from there.

The serpent said of the fruit "that in the day you eat from it your eyes will be opened, and you will be like God" (Gen. 3:5). Sin is an action we take to be independent of God Himself. Sin makes us into little gods, living our lives as we please, not taking into account what the Master Designer has said is best for us. Sin exalts our own reasoning abilities above what God has said. The crafty serpent began to rationalize with Eve. This is what we often do today. We rationalize matters until doing what God has said not to do appears perfectly acceptable to us. However, human reasoning, while important, is faulty. The Lord said "The heart is more deceitful than all else, and is desperately sick—who can understand it? I, the Lord, search the heart; I test the mind, even to give to each man according to his ways, according to the results of his deeds" (Jer. 17:9–10).

Often, people will say, "Just trust your heart." However, based upon the above Scripture, this is not a wise thing to do. Our hearts often lead us astray. Since the fall of humanity in the Garden of Eden, we are all infected with the sin disease, and the only cure is Jesus Christ. He alone can redeem the human heart and make it into His likeness.

You may still be questioning the validity of the ancient manuscripts of Scripture, and whether or not you can trust them. The discovery of the Dead Sea Scrolls by a shepherd boy in a cave in 1947 should help alleviate your doubts. These original manuscripts "contain at least parts of every Old Testament book except Esther…most important, they confirm the reliability of the Masoretic text, the most reliable Hebrew text we have."[45]

Begin to read the Bible as God's trustworthy canon of truth by which you can live. If you have not been an avid reader of Scripture, I suggest you begin in the beginning with the book of Genesis and begin to enjoy the exciting adventure of reading about God's involvement with humankind throughout history. As you read, I encourage you to ask God to reveal His truths to you. It is for sure He can be trusted, and there is no need to dispute His word. He has your best interest at heart!

---

[45] Bill T. Arnold and Bryan E. Beyer, 2008, *Encountering the Old Testament (Encountering Biblical Studies*, Grand Rapids, MI: Baker Academic.

CULT

What comes to mind when you think of a cult? Perhaps, it is a certain wild clothing style that the members adopt or the communal living characteristic of some cults. Who remembers the horrific scenes of the 1970s from Guyana, where hundreds of followers of Jim Jones took their lives by drinking poison as we see these bodies lying side by side, face down in the dirt? Perhaps you recall the tragic deaths of thirty-nine members of the Heaven's Gate cult in the 1990s, when the bodies of these cult members were found dead inside a California mansion. Maybe the images of David Koresh and the Branch Davidians come to mind, as you see the standoff between this group and the ATF, and the ultimate raid by the ATF on this group. Whatever image comes to mind, it is for certain that you want to avoid such beliefs and behavior.

However, do all cults portray bizarre beliefs and behavior? Do all cults withdraw from the culture and portray a strange lifestyle that is out of the norm from the rest of society? What defines an organization as a cult? How can you identify a group as a cult? While there may be multiple characteristics that define an organization as a cult, there is one area that provides a distinguishing factor between a cult and a legitimate religion. We represent that factor as follows:

    C—Christ
    U—Undermined and
    L—Limited
    T—Theologically

How an organization views Jesus Christ and His nature, identity, function, and authority reveals whether or not an organization is a cult or false religion.

No one disputes the historical fact that a Galilean by the name of Jesus lived in Palestine from around AD 0 until AD 33. He taught during a three-year ministry, gathered disciples unto Himself, and ultimately, was executed on a cross for what the political and religious leaders of the day deemed insurrection. His body was placed in a borrowed tomb, and days later, the tomb was empty. His followers, first of which were women, made claims of His appearances to them following the fact. His followers claim He rose from the dead, and eleven of twelve of His apostles eventually died for making the resurrection claim. His antagonists make other claims as to what happened to His body. However, the body has never been found. I submit that if Jesus Christ was resurrected from the dead He is God Himself, the Son of God as He claimed, the Savior, and Lord of all.

First, let us examine His nature. The Bible says in the gospel of John chapter 1

> In the beginning was the Word, and the Word was with God, and the Word was God. He was in the beginning with God. All things came into being through Him, and apart from Him nothing came into being that has come into being.

This Scripture passage tells us that the Word, Jesus Himself, was God. The apostle John goes on to say that Jesus was in the beginning with God and that all things were made through Jesus. Furthermore, Jesus said "I and the Father are one" (John 10:30). Any organization that does not claim that Jesus Christ is divine in nature and God Himself is a false religion. There are some who will argue that Jesus never made the claim to be God. In John 10:30 above, one can see this is not true. Jesus did claim to be God, and He was and is God. The fact Jesus was with God in the beginning proves that He is not a created being. Instead, He is the Creator. In the Old Testament, God said "Let *Us* make man in *Our* image, according to *Our* likeness" (Gen. 1:26 italics added). God the Father, God the Son, and God the Holy Spirit have existed forever, and it is this Trinity that created the world and everything in it.

Second, let us examine His person or identity. Jesus often refers to God as His Father, indicating that He made the claim to be the Son of God. God Himself identified Jesus as His Son both at Jesus's baptism (Matt. 3:17) and during the transfiguration by stating "This is my beloved Son, with whom I am well pleased" (Matt. 17:5). God Himself endorsed Jesus as His Son, validating the fact that Jesus was more than a prophet and a teacher. He was, in fact, the Son of God, and God was pleased with Him. Any religion that claims that Jesus Christ is anything less than the Son of God is a false religion.

Third, let us look to Jesus's function or why he came to earth. It was Matthew who recorded in his gospel "For he will save his people from their sins" (Matt. 1:21). Jesus's very purpose in leaving His Father in heaven and coming to earth was to go to the cross and make payment for the sins of humanity. And He was the only One who could atone, or pay, for our sins. Today, there are even some "Christian" organizations who do not want to emphasize the Christ's payment for sin. These organizations seem to gloss over the cross, as if it were an incidental happening. However, the cross is central to the reason that Jesus came to earth. All through the Old Testament, we find that sin had to be atoned, or paid for, by the blood of animal sacrifices. However, with the sin payment Jesus made, the "blood of bulls and goats" would no longer be needed to remove sins. Jesus Christ made the final payment for sins, and this was decreed in the eternal counsel of God. Any organization that does not claim Jesus is the only savior from humanity's sins is a false religion.

Fourth, let us examine Jesus's authority. The apostle Paul wrote concerning Jesus in Colossians 1:16–19

> For by Him all things were created,
> both in the heavens and on earth, visible

and invisible, whether thrones or dominions or rulers or authorities—all things have been created through Him and for Him. He is before all things, and in Him all things hold together. He is also head of the body, the church; and He is the beginning, the firstborn from the dead, so that He Himself will come to have first place in everything. For it was the Father's good pleasure for all the fulness to dwell in Him.

In these verses, the apostle Paul writes that Jesus is the Creator, Sustainer, Resurrected One, and God Himself. He uses a word that asserts that Jesus has the final authority, preeminent, which means in the original Greek "to have the first place." Jesus's rightful authority in all the universe and in our lives is to have the first place. The apostle Paul wrote in another book "So that at the name of Jesus every knee will bow, of those who are in heaven and on earth and under the earth, and that every tongue will confess that Jesus Christ is Lord, to the glory of God the Father" (Phil. 2:10–11). Jesus Himself said that He has the authority to "raise up on the last day" (John 6:40) those who believe in Him. Jesus Christ is Lord! Any religion that claims any less is a false religion.

We can clearly see through Scripture that Jesus Christ is divine in His nature, the sinless Son of God in His person, the Savior from sins in His function, and Lord in His authority. Jesus said "I am the way, the truth, and the life.

No one comes to the Father but through Me" (John 14:6)." How is it with you? Who do you say Jesus is? Jesus asked Simon Peter the same question as recorded in Matthew 16:15–17, and Peter's response was "You are the Christ, the Son of the living God."

Following Peter's response, Jesus said, "Blessed are you, Simon Bar Jonah, because flesh and blood did not reveal this to you, but my Father who is in heaven" (v. 17).

During the course of reading this chapter, has God revealed the true identity of His Son to you? If so, talk to Jesus Christ. God's word assures that "whoever will call on the name of the Lord will be saved" (Rom. 10:13). Talk to Jesus right now where you are and be saved from the false notions that prevail in our society today about who Jesus is and what constitutes the path to God. You will not regret it in this life or in the eternal life to come!

THE BATTLES WITHIN

My oldest son was three years old when I heard the following words coming incessantly from his mouth, as he stood in the corner of time out for having done something he should not have done, "I don't know why I do it, but I always do it. I don't want to do it, but I do it anyway." He kept repeating this over and over through sobs of remorse. He defined the human condition very well, even at age three. Could this be a future theologian in the making? It's reminiscent of what the apostle Paul said about his own struggles "For what I am doing, I do not understand; for I am not practicing what I would like to do, but I am doing the very thing I hate" (Rom. 7: 15).

Whether verbalized from a three-year-old or the apostle Paul, the message is the same. As humans, each of us have battles with which we engage on a daily basis. For the Christian, it is the battle between the old human nature and the new nature in Christ. Upon conversion, we are given a new nature that desires to please God. However, we still battle the desires to please ourselves. This happens between the "now and not yet" of our lives. We are redeemed from the power of sin now. However, we are not yet free from the presence of sin and will not be completely free from the presence of sin until we find ourselves completely in God's presence in heaven.

So what are we to do? Give up and quit and simply give in to the desires that are not pleasing to God? The intensity of the battle is real! The desires of the flesh are ever present. This can be discouraging to a follower of Christ who "is a new creature" (2 Cor. 5:17). It can be discouraging to one who has surrendered his/her life to Christ, thinking that all will be well in the future.

I would suggest that the internal struggles that a Christian has between the old sinful nature and the new Christ nature is one piece of evidence that indicates that person has truly been redeemed by the Son of God. If one were simply giving oneself over to sinful desires without a struggle, this would indicate no desire to please the One who died and rose again on one's behalf. The very fact that a struggle exists indicates that one no longer desires to please himself/herself, but the One who saves.

In Paul's letter to Titus, he wrote "For the grace of God has appeared, bringing salvation to all men, instructing us to deny ungodliness and worldly passions, and to live sensibly, upright, and godly lives in the present age" (Titus 2:11–12). The grace of God is free to those who will receive it. However, those who have been embraced by God's grace in Christ Jesus are called upon to live lives that honor the One who has embraced them.

Whether or not we live lives that honor Christ depends on what dwells in the heart. It was the Lord Himself who said "For out of the heart come evil thoughts, murders, adulteries, sexual immorality, thefts, false witness, slanders" (Matt. 15:19). Our inner struggles eventually manifest themselves outwardly, if not properly dealt with. It was former president Jimmy Carter who, on the campaign trail in 1976 was asked by reporters if he had ever committed adultery, replied, "I've looked on a lot of women with lust. I've committed adultery in my heart many times."[46] Regardless of one's estimation of his presidency, we must acknowledge that he certainly answered in an honest and transparent manner concerning his inner battle.

Jesus Christ indicated that sins like murder and adultery begin in the heart. He taught much about the importance of the heart, the very essence of a person. He said "For the mouth speaks out of that which fills the heart" (Matt. 12:34, NASB). We can see how important it is to tend to matters of the heart. It was the prophet Jeremiah who proclaimed "The heart is deceitful above all things." Therefore, we must be careful to examine our heart and guard it for "everything you do flows from it" (Prov. 4:23, NIV). This is not popular truth for today's current post-modern culture. However, it is truth, nonetheless, because it is spoken by the Author of truth, God Himself.

The Author of life and eternal life through the risen, Jesus Christ, knows what is best when it comes to living a joyful life. We must be careful which nature we feed because the reality is that whichever nature we feed will be the one that wins the battles fought within. Which nature are you feeding? Is it the old, sinful nature, or the new nature Christ imparted to you upon conversion? We know

---

[46] "Carter's Comments on Sex Cause Concern," *New York Times*, accessed December 9, 2019, https://www.nytimes.com/1976/09/23/archives/carters-comments-on-sex-cause-concern.html.

who will ultimately bring the victory in the "not yet" (Rom. 7:25), and He can bring the victory in the "now," if we feed on the truths that He provides in His word and through the power of the Holy Spirit.

TRUE WORSHIP

Corporate worship is deeply rooted in the New Testament and has foundations that go all the way back to Old Testament times. We are told in Hebrews "And let us consider how to stimulate one another to love and good deeds, not forsaking our own assembling together, as is the habit of some, but encouraging one another; and all the more as you see the day drawing near" (Heb. 10:24–25). We see from this passage that one vital reason for gathering often as a group of Christ followers is to encourage each other. We draw strength in the fellowship of believers. The result of effective worship should be as the writer of Hebrews says in verse 24 above, "to promote love and good deeds." Worship is about fulfilling the purpose of God during our time on this earth. What occurs as we worship together is that we get fueled up for the week ahead, so we can go into the workplace and community in "love and good works" and draw attention to Jesus, who has saved us. Jesus, our pattern, made it a habit to worship corporately with others as we see recorded by Luke, "*As was His custom*, He entered the synagogue on the Sabbath day" (Luke 4:16). If the perfect Savior made a habit of participating in corporate worship, then certainly we need to do the same!

You may ask, what did early Christians do when they gathered together? Colossians 3:16 gives us some insight. Paul writes "Let the word of Christ richly dwell within you, with all wisdom teaching and admonishing one another with psalms and hymns and spiritual songs, singing with thankfulness in your hearts to God." This verse gives us the content of what happened when early Christians gathered together. However, in the verses preceding this, we see that a right relationship with other believers precedes the gathering. We are told by Paul, in verse 13 of the same chapter, how to treat each other. He says such things as "bearing with one another and forgiving each other" and "just as the Lord forgave you, so also should you." This gives a clear indication that our relationships with fellow Christians must be right for corporate worship to be all that God intends.

Given that our relationships are right with each other, what are we to do once we gather? The first part of verse 16 is clear, the message about Jesus must be the focal point of all we do. Paul writes that that message should "richly dwell within you." Make no mistake, everything we do in worship should point to Jesus. Christ Jesus alone makes worship of God possible because of what He did on the cross and through His resurrection. Without Jesus, there is no true worship. Thus, in all the songs we sing and the sermons we preach, Jesus Christ must take first place in everything.

Paul then writes that we gather corporately in order to "teach and admonish one another." We gather to learn the truths of God's word. There has been no other time in history when the Bible has been more readily available. We gather to delve deeply into this Word and be strengthened in the faith. We also gather to be admonished. In Greek, *admonish* means "reasoning with someone by warning."[47] We gather together not to feel good about ourselves. Instead, we gather to be warned by the pastor and others. Why would we need someone to reason with us by issuing a warning? We need this because, even though the blood of Jesus has redeemed us, we still live in a fallen world, where we battle the world, the flesh, and the devil. Thus, we need someone to warn us of the pitfalls of sin, lest we fall into its sinister trap. We see from this emphasis that the Word of God, which is completely true, must take center stage in a corporate worship service to help us counter the lies of the world, the flesh, and the devil.

We also see from Colossians 3:16 that we are to sing together in worship of Christ. Let's look at the content of the singing. In the early church, the songs were of three types. First, the early believers sang psalms. That is, they would sing Scripture (Psalms from the Old Testament book) set to music. In this way, believers were reminded of truths straight from God's word. Second, they sang hymns, songs of celebration and praise to a triune God. Worship was a joyful occasion where believers in Jesus got the opportunity to praise the risen Savior together. Finally, they sang spiritual songs. Spiritual songs were spontaneous, impromptu, unrehearsed melodies of praise to God from a Spirit-filled heart. Thus, there was a dependence on the Holy Spirit

---

[47] Strong's Exhaustive Concordance," Biblehub.com, accessed December 12, 2019, https://biblehub.com/greek/3560.htm.

in the gatherings of early Christians to direct their worship and give them what they needed to adequately express themselves to the Father. We need that same dependence on the Holy Spirit today.

Paul concludes verse 16 by telling us how we are to sing as we worship the Lord Jesus. We are instructed to sing *with gratitude*. A heart of gratitude recognizes God as the Creator, Sustainer, and Giver of all things. A heart of gratitude acknowledges that God is the One who gives the free gift of eternal life through Jesus Christ His Son. It is with this attitude of gratitude that we are to sing to God. The true worshipper of Christ recognizes there is nothing good within us; whereby, we can claim the right to worship God. Conversely, the true worshipper of Christ recognizes that Christ alone is worthy and has paved the way for us to have access to the God of the universe through what He did on the cross and in the resurrection from the dead.

Notice that Paul said that we are to sing with gratitude *in our hearts*. True worship comes from the depth of one's being. We are to be genuine when we sing to God. You can mouth words and not really think about or sincerely mean what you sing. However, Paul instructs us to sing in our hearts to God. Old Testament worshippers caused God's displeasure when they worshipped God only out of routine. Jesus quoted Isaiah when he was speaking to the Pharisees and scribes and said "You hypocrites, rightly did Isaiah prophesy of you: 'This people honors me with their lips, but their heart is far away from me. But in vain do they worship Me, teaching as doctrines the precepts of men'" (Matt 15:7–9). We must be sure when we worship

God that the worship flows from deep within and that our hearts agree with the words our lips proclaim, or else we are worshipping in vain. Genuine worship comes from the heart.

Finally, Paul instructs the church to sing *to God*. On the surface, this might seem obvious. However, it is important to remember when we worship corporately that we sing not to please others or ourselves. The whole reason we sing is to make much of the God who has redeemed us through Christ. We are not only to sing *about* God, we are to sing *to* God. The worship pastor is only a prompter in worship, providing a framework within which every believer can engage in genuine worship of God "in spirit and truth" (John 4:24).

LIVING LIFE BLINDLY

Do no love the world nor the things in the world. If anyone loves the world, the love of the Father is not in him. For all that is in the world, the lust of the flesh and the lust of the eyes and the boastful pride of life, is not from the Father, but is from the world.
—John 2: 15–16

I have often been amazed at the abilities of people for whom the light of day is dim or nonexistent. I have been impressed with their ability to navigate the world from what many perceive as a handicap. I became amazed in an up-close-and-personal way by an elementary school music teacher who happened to be blind. Blind from birth and the child of caring parents, this music teacher indeed benefited from excellent schooling through the years. However, what she possessed went far beyond the training that she had received.

This music teacher possessed a keen intellect, sense of humor, and a determined spirit to navigate the complexities of life with success and to do anything that a perfectly sighted person could do. Not wanting sympathy, but appreciative of the thoughtfulness of others, this teacher managed and, to this day (twenty years later), still skillfully manages and teaches multiple classrooms of students daily all by herself! You may wonder what has contributed to this successful teaching career. I believe it is her ability to work within the parameters of what has been dealt to her by life and to make the most of every day within those parameters.

I think the blind may see things more clearly than those of us who have excellent vision. They realize there are limits to what they can do. However, they do not let those limits keep them from becoming all they were intended to be. All of us, even those with twenty-twenty vision have limits. It is simply a part of the human condition. However, the best approach to life is to accept those limits, but not allow them to become excuses. Far too many of us focus so much on the limits we never fulfill the God-given potential inherent within each of us. Perhaps it was Edward Everett Hale who put it best when he said, "I cannot do everything, but still I can do something and because I cannot do everything, I will not refuse to do the something I can do."[48] We would do well to have this kind of sentiment when approaching life.

In addition to being "limit-busters," perhaps many of those who are blind realize what is really important in life. Not having the luxury of being able to see the obvious in the world, they must have an additional sense with which to navigate life. Blind people are not concerned with appearances, like so many of the rest of us. It is not the value of the clothes one is wearing. It is the value of the heart with which one is communicating that matters.

---

[48] Forbes Quotes Thoughts on the Business of Life, accessed December 12, 2019, https://www.forbes.com/quotes/2504/

They know who is truly listening to them in a conversation because they have honed the skill of listening. By the same token, they are able to fully concentrate on what the other person is communicating because they are not distracted like the rest of us, who are so prone in this world of technology to allow the cell phone or computer ding to carry our attention away from the conversation at hand.

There are some things that just don't matter to the blind. Those things include outward beauty and strength, splendor and perfection of one's home, fashion and stylishness of one's clothes, comparison of self with other people, type of car one has, and possessions in general. The things that do matter to the visually impaired include *inward* beauty and strength, *relationships* within one's home, functionality of one's home, the practical nature of one's clothes, and the realization that a car's true value is in the reliability of getting one from point A to point B.

Let's illustrate it this way. Can you imagine a blind person attending a beauty pageant? What would be most important for a blind person to sense about the contestants? Obviously, it would not be the sleek beauty of the contestants or the perfection of their hair and makeup. I wonder how different the outcome of a beauty pageant would be if blind people were the judges. Please do not misunderstand. There is nothing inherently wrong with outward beauty, as it is a gift from the Creator God. However, blind people know something that the rest of us often forget. Beauty is a much more complex issue than simply what is on the surface. Beauty is in the heart of the one being beheld.

Many of us sighted individuals are somewhat like the Pharisees during Jesus's day. We put far too much emphasis on the outward appearance and ignore the qualities of the inner person, which are most important. Jesus reserved His strongest words for the "religious" Pharisees. He said "Woe to you, scribes and Pharisees, hypocrites! For you are like whitewashed tombs which on the outside appear beautiful, but inside they are full of dead's men's bones and all uncleanness. So, you, too, outwardly appear righteous to men, but inwardly you are full of hypocrisy and lawlessness" (Matt. 23:27–28). The Pharisees had perfect physical vision. They had studied, observed, and even taught others from the Torah. However, Jesus referred to them as "blind guides" (Matt. 23:24). You see, even though they were religious and taught others to be religious, they were blind. They did not realize that Jesus had come to redeem the human heart from its sinful motives and not just clean up a person on the outside.

Finally, the physically blind have a healthy dependence upon other people. They allow others to transport them from one place to another. Sometimes, they also allow a person, service dog, or cane help them navigate locations. We would all do well to learn from this. There are times in life when we all need help from others to move us along. It is foolish to believe or act otherwise. Sometimes, we are the helper, and sometimes, we are the person who needs the help. We need each other.

Furthermore, we also need Jesus. You may say, "Well, I'm not very religious." I have good news for you. Jesus did not come for the religious. He came for those who recognize they have a need and need His help. We could learn from the visually impaired here and recognize that to get from Point A, earth, to Point B, heaven, we need One greater than us. We need the God-man, who surrendered His life on the Roman instrument of execution, a cross. His death served as payment for the sins of anyone who will receive Him as the free gift of eternal life.

So don't be like the Pharisees who looked so good on the outside that they forgot to address the inside. They had twenty-twenty vision physically, but they were spiritually blind. Be more like those who are physically blind and realize that what is on the inside of a person is what really matters. It's what matters in life, and it's what matters for eternal life. Can't you see?

IT'S THE MESSAGE, NOT METHODS (WHEN IT COMES TO BECOMING A CHRISTIAN)

If you grew up in conservative Christian circles like I did, it is likely that you were exposed to lots of ideas concerning just the right formula for one to be truly saved and become a part of God's kingdom. For some, it may have been walking an aisle, praying a prescribed prayer, begging for mercy, praying through, being baptized, or being confirmed. Many claimed then, and some claim now, that unless you do one or more of the previously mentioned acts, Jesus Christ has not redeemed you. The problem with this line of thinking by many well-intentioned and sincere people is that it *overemphasizes* what the person does and *underemphasizes* what God does in saving people.

In order to determine what is truly essential to be saved, we must look to the founder of Christianity, Jesus Himself. It seems logical to look at what Jesus said when He began His ministry. The gospel of Mark records the following

> And after John had been taken into custody, Jesus came into Galilee, preach-

ing the gospel of God, and saying 'The time is fulfilled, and the kingdom of God is at hand; repent and believe in the gospel. (Mark 1:14–15, NASB)

We read here the essentials of becoming a Christ follower. The Greek meaning of the word *repent* is "to think differently" or "reconsider."[49] Jesus is saying that to become His follower, we must think differently about sin, life, and our relationship to God. He says we must acknowledge that the way we have been approaching life is not working. We must do an "about face." We must turn from sin and self. He then shows us to whom we must turn, Himself. He says we must believe in the gospel. The gospel is the good news that He came to redeem fallen mankind through His death on the cross and His bodily resurrection. In Greek, the word *believe* means "to entrust."[50] Therefore, we must entrust ourselves to Jesus, and that what He did in becoming our substitute on the cross was sufficient to pay for our sins, and that what He did through the resurrection was sufficient to ensure eternal life for us.

In essence, Jesus tells us that what we do in repentance and faith is to put the focus on Him. It is He who did the dying, so we might live. He does not ask us to do something to earn our way to Him. He does not ask us to do something to put the focus on ourselves. Instead, He asks us to turn from sin and admit that we need His forgiveness

---

[49] "Strong's Concordance," biblehub.com, accessed December 14, 2019, https://biblehub.com/greek/3340.htm.
[50] Ibid.

and to look to Him, the only One who can forgive sin. He asks us to entrust ourselves to Him, the only One who can provide eternal life.

No leader of any other religion can make the claim that He died and rose again from the dead. In fact, other religions basically claim that by doing good deeds, one can earn acceptance with God, or whom they deem to be God. This ignores the grace of the true and living God who did the work for human beings. Under the inspiration of the Holy Spirit, the apostle Paul writes "For by grace you have been saved through faith; and that not of yourselves, it is the *gift of God;* not as a result of works, that no one may boast" (Ephes. 2:8–9). God grants salvation as a gift from Him. Therefore, we are to live "to the praise of His glory" (Ephes. 1). God never intended that salvation be something we earn. He knew that would lead to boasting on our part, and He only wants our boasting to be in Him.

One becomes a redeemed follower of Jesus when the Father draws that person to Himself. Jesus said "No one can come to Me unless the Father who sent Me draws him; and I will raise him up on the last day" (John 6:44). We see here that God initiates the work of salvation and will bring that work to completion. Jesus made a promise here that the one whom the Father draws will be raised up on the last day. All of Jesus's promises are true. God ensures by His drawing power that those in whom He is at work will come to Jesus Christ through repentance and believing in Him. Jesus said "This is the work of God, that you believe in Him whom He has sent" (John 6:29).

However, even for those who believe that salvation is "by grace through faith," methods have been added and these methods have unwittingly put the focus on the individual instead of God, and God will share His glory with no one. Sure, there must be a way for one who has been born again to let people know publicly he or she is now an unashamed follower of Jesus Christ. That is what one does when he or she is baptized publicly. However, even in baptism, the focus is on the death, burial, and resurrection of Jesus, as the believer is symbolically buried in believer's baptism and raised to walk in newness of life.

Dear reader, do you sense that God is at work in your life, drawing you to Himself and the truth of who His Son, Jesus, really is? If you do, go ahead and repent of your sin and believe in the good news that Jesus Christ has done what is necessary for you to be forgiven and have eternal life through Him. You will never be the same because of *His* work in you!

WANT TO MAKE THE WORLD A BETTER PLACE? LOOK IN THE MIRROR!

It was the late 1980s, and the singer was Michael Jackson backed up by the Winans and a gospel choir. It was an upbeat, catchy tune that went like this, "I'm starting with the man in the mirror, I'm asking him to change his ways, and no message could have been any clearer, if you wanna make the world a better place, take a look at yourself, and then make a change."[51]

Many of us tend to be quite idealistic when we are young. We think that we can change the world. Therefore, we set out preparing for a profession that will allow us to impact people's lives in a positive way. We may even begin the process by volunteering in the community or at church. We can certainly not fault these lofty ambitions or actions. After all, these actions are selfless. However, sometimes before we set out to change the world, we need to do as the song suggests, "take a look at yourself and make a change." You see, one of the best gifts you can give other people is a better you!

---

[51] Jackson, Michael, 1987, "Man in the Mirror," *Bad*, album.

Serving others will have a greater impact when the you that is offered to them is the best you that you can be. In order to do this, one must be willing to examine one's self. It was Socrates who said, "The unexamined life is not worth living."[52] He was right! We must be willing to be introspective enough to see our faults and allow the God who made us to help us correct them.

This process takes courage because it can be very uncomfortable. We do not like seeing our flaws and, often, would rather identify the flaws of others than our very own. Jesus refers to this as "speck removing." Okay, He didn't exactly use that language, but that is what He meant. He said "Why do you see the speck that is in your brother's eye, but do not notice the log that is in your own eye?" (Matt. 7:3). He urges the removing of the log in your own eye, so you can see clearly enough to remove your brother's speck. When we go through this uncomfortable process with ourselves, we will have the needed humility to help a fellow traveler.

I had a rude awakening to this when I was in high school. I will never forget the day. I was in third period choir class, and the class had not actually begun yet. I was visiting with my friend, and we were chatting about where some of our other friends were going the following weekend. I made some kind of comment about how they would be partying the whole time. She said to me, "You are too judgmental." This was a blunt message that began a change process in my life. I realized the four words she

---

[52] Quote, Wikipedia, accessed December 14, 2019, https://en.wikipedia.org/wiki/The_unexamined_life_is_not_worth_living.

said to me were true. The words hurt at first, but the more I thought about what she said, the more I realized I was living a self-righteous life of condemning other people. First of all, righteousness is not good if it is self-righteousness. Secondly, the pride I had was beneficial to no one. It was time for me to look at myself and make a change.

What about you? Are you open to examining your life? What would it take for you to be willing to take a good look at yourself? We are talking about examining your motives about why you behave a certain way. This also takes an examination of your actions and, especially, words to see whom they benefit. For example, how many of your comments refer to the behavior of other people? How many times do you use the word *I* in conversation with other people? These are telling signs of your current attitude toward yourself and others.

If you are not able to ascertain your current condition, ask someone with whom you live. If you are married, your spouse will be an excellent choice to give feedback. Whomever you ask, make sure it is someone who only has your best interest at heart. Do not ask someone with whom you have a relationship that is already rocky. Ask someone with whom you have had a solid relationship for some time. However, I must issue this warning. Do not ask someone else to give you feedback unless you are willing to accept the feedback without defending yourself. We seem to have an innate defense mechanism when it comes to getting candid feedback that is not flattering to us. However, getting feedback from others may be the only way that true change begins to happen.

The human condition is that we have certain blind spots in our lives. These are areas of our lives we truly do not have the capacity within ourselves with which to deal. The only way for light to be shed on these areas is for someone else to expose the blind spot and make us aware. It is what the psalmist alludes to when he prays "Who can discern his errors? Acquit me of hidden faults" (Psalm 90:12). In essence, he is saying to God, "God, I admit there are areas of my life that have fault lines that only You know. Please cleanse me from these faults." The psalmist is willing to be exposed. We, too, must be willing to have our faults exposed, if change is to occur in our lives.

I came to the realization a long time ago that the only person I can change with certainty is myself. And this is a lifelong process. The Christian term for it is sanctification. Sanctification means God is working in you to make you more like His Son. This is His goal for someone that has come to saving faith in Jesus Christ. This goal will not be reached as long as we are constantly removing specks from the lives of other people. However, as we examine our own lives for "planks," God begins to teach us and to form a better person in the image of His Son. As this happens, we become better able to serve others in a way that is authentic and believable.

Jesus had a word for people who fail to examine their own faults before helping others. The word is hypocrite (Matt. 7:5). It comes from a Greek word, meaning "actor, like a performer acting under a mask."[53] Jesus actually stated

---

[53] Strong's Concordance, biblehub.com, accessed December 14, 2019, https://biblehub.com/greek/5273.htm.

this describes someone who looks for flaws in the lives of others but fails to consider one's own flaws. However, when you lead a life of self-examination, great things begin to happen. You are a better father, mother, son, daughter, employer, employee, volunteer, teacher, leader, etc.

Then, what begins to happen is you are able to influence people in a positive life-giving way. The values you exhibit are consistent with the core of who you are because you have allowed the Creator of your core to form you as He wishes. These values are not only taught; they are caught by everyone with whom you spend time. They see the sermon lived out before them on a regular basis. And it speaks. You speak, but more importantly, God speaks through you because you have allowed Him to speak in you. It is a quite exciting journey! Are you ready? Take a look at yourself and then make a change.

YOUR DAYS ARE NUMBERED

You and I will not live forever. It is an understood conclusion that each of us born on this earth will one day leave this earth. We do not know when that day will arrive, but it is certain it will. Now, before you think that I am trying to lead you into an existential abyss, I will make my point. The whole reason to think about the limited number of days we have is to put more life into those days. When we realize that we will not live forever on this earth, we can seek to live the days we do have with more wisdom and joy.

Moses wrote in a prayer to God "so teach us to number our days, that we may present to You a heart of wisdom." The first thing we notice about this verse is that we have to be taught. It does not come natural for us to think about the finiteness of life, and it may be an uncomfortable thing for us to do. However, it is a worthwhile activity. The original Hebrew word for *number* in this sentence is *manah*. It means to "count or reckon."[54]

The Hebrew meaning of the word implies we are to carefully think about the number of days in our lives. This is not a difficult activity. However, it can be sobering. For example, at the time of this writing, I am nearly fifty-two

---

[54] Strong's Concordance, biblehub.com, accessed December 14, 2019, https://biblehub.com/hebrew/4487.htm.

years old. I have been alive approximately 18,980 days. Should I be blessed enough to live until 70 years of age, that will be 18 more years, or 6,570 days. That is less than half the days I have already lived. This was quite illuminating to me!

So now, you try it! It's not difficult. Get online and go to www.numberyourdays.com.[55] This website will perform the calculation for you. You can enter any date and find out how long it has been since that date, and you can also enter any date in the future and find out how long it will be until that day arrives. Put down this book and start calculating, and then come back and read the rest of this chapter.

How long do you have? This is a question often associated with someone who has a terminal disease. However, we are all terminal. We may not be afflicted with a terminal disease, but each of us has an expiration date. Now that you know how many days you could have left if blessed enough to continue living, what will you change? What will you do differently?

You see, meditating on the brevity of life tends to refocus our priorities. Is there someone you need to forgive? Is there someone from whom you need to *seek* forgiveness? Is there a relationship that needs repair or restoration? Are there people with whom you need to invest more time? Are there debts that need to be paid? Are there goals that need to be written? Are there steps that need to be taken to reach those goals? Do you need to set aside money to reach an important objective? Do you need to make preparation for eternity? Whatever the issue is *now* is the time to take

---

[55] http://numberyourdays.com/.

action. Days are flying by. Listen to the wisdom of James when he writes "You are just a vapor that appears for a little while and then vanishes away" (James 4:14).

Now, someone may read this and say, "Okay, I know that I don't have very long so I am going to just 'eat, drink, and be merry' and enjoy the time that I do have left." However, there really is a problem with this perspective. It only benefits one person—the person with the self-indulgent attitude. John Donne told us many years ago, "No man is an island entire of itself."[56] Our actions indeed affect other people—family, friends, coworkers, and acquaintances—all within our sphere of influence. So the self-indulgent attitude may indeed temporarily benefit the one who possesses this attitude, but it also may harm those whom the person loves. Therefore, this "live only for pleasure" approach is not a viable option!

In fact, a very wise man once wrote, "It is better to go to a house of mourning than to go to a house of feasting, because that is the end of every man, and the living takes it to heart" (Eccle. 7:2). Oddly enough, Solomon writes that it is better to take counsel from those who are grieving the death of someone they love than to take counsel from those who are reveling in their pleasures. The idea here is that those who are mourning realize what is actually important in life because of the events that now shape their perspective. This is the opposite of the wisdom that we see offered by many in the world today. However, it is truth, nonetheless. As we live our lives each day, the memories and legacy

---

[56] "No Man is an Island," Scottish Poetry Library, accessed December 14, 2019, https://www.scottishpoetrylibrary.org.uk/poem/no-man-is-an-island/.

we leave behind for those who remain after we are gone need to become primary in our thoughts and actions.

Our lives may be a shooting star in comparison with all eternity. However, we can make the choice to burn brightly as we make our streak in time. Number your days and make each one of them count for the good of mankind and the glory of God who made you.

HIS MERCIES ARE NEW EVERY MORNING

One of the most refreshing thoughts for human beings is that each day we get to begin again. No matter what took place the day before, however bad it may have been, the sunrise brings a new opportunity to start over. It was God Himself, in all His wisdom, who instituted the very concept of time "and there was evening and there was morning, one day" (Gen. 1:5). He knew that we would need these opportunities for new beginnings, so he structured time to facilitate this.

A passage of Scripture that especially speaks to this concept is Lamentations 3:22–23 "His compassions never fail. They are new every morning." It is so comforting that as human beings, prone to mistakes and sin, we have an amazing God who is full of mercy. The very fact that you are reading this means His mercies are abundant toward you because you are experiencing a new day He has created.

The only appropriate response in appreciation for His extended mercies is rejoicing. Psalm 118:24 says "This is the day which the Lord has made; let us rejoice and be glad in it." Notice what the psalmist does *not* say. He does not say let us be downcast and sad. He says the very fact that

God has allowed us to be a part of something He has created should cause us to radiate God's joy.

The secret to rejoicing in the mercies each day brings is trusting in God's character. We can know, no matter what happens, God is faithful. The Lamentations passage speaks to this. The first part of verse 22 says "The Lord's lovingkindnesses indeed never cease," and latter half of verse 23 says "Great is your faithfulness." The reason we can rejoice in each day is because of the faithful character of God.

In verse 23, the Hebrew meaning of *faithfulness* refers to firmness, steadfastness, and fidelity.[57] God will not cheat you! There is never a time when He will abandon you. People are fickle and not always trustworthy. This is not an issue with God. He is committed to you, even when you are not committed to Him. Therefore, we can rejoice in His mercies each day, knowing He cares for us with the greatest of tenderness and fidelity.

As we daily rejoice in God's mercies, we can impart His mercies to others as well. When we are cut off in traffic, insulted by an angry stranger, or in conflict with a family member, we can respond in these situations out of the abundance of His mercies. However, we cannot respond correctly unless we have spent time basking in His mercies. We must begin each day reminded of the mercies of God by spending time with Him and refreshing our minds and spirits with His word and in conversation with Him. When we do this, His mercies cannot help but flow in us and through us to others.

---

[57] Strong's Concordance, biblehub.com, accessed December 14, 2019, https://biblehub.com/hebrew/530.htm.

We also must keep in mind that we cannot be merciful to others, unless we are merciful with ourselves as well. Too many of us beat up on ourselves for past mistakes and wallow in these to the point of losing our ability to be merciful to others. We must adopt the attitude of the apostle Paul, who did not consider himself to have achieved it all. Instead, he did one thing. He forgot the past and "reached forward to what lies ahead" (Phil. 3:13). This is what makes for good mental health and merciful treatment of self and others!

Although I certainly do not agree with the tenets of transcendentalism, I like what Ralph Waldo Emerson said when he wrote, "Finish each day and be done with it. You have done what you could. Some blunders and absurdities no doubt crept in; forget them as soon as you can. Tomorrow is a new day. You shall begin it serenely and with too high a spirit to be encumbered with your old nonsense."[58] Now, if Ralph Waldo Emerson, who did not believe in the God of the Bible, could have this healthy perspective, we, as Christians, who know the mercies of God should be able to forget past blunders and move on to the future.

Therefore, bask in the mercies God provides each day. Drink deeply from His well of living waters and allow your soul to be restored. Then, become a *mercy dispenser* to others with whom you come into contact each day. Remember "mercy triumphs over judgment" (James 2:13). Be a victor through mercy!

---

[58] Quotable Quote, Goodreads, accessed December 14, 2019, https://www.goodreads.com/quotes/18830-finish-each-day-and-be-done-with-it-you-have.

EXCUSE ME, CAN YOU TELL ME WHAT IS THE MEANING OF LIFE?

I was a freshman in college when I was awakened at four-thirty, one Sunday morning in my dorm room by the phone ringing. When I picked up the phone (in those days we still had landlines), I heard music and conversation in the background, and the person on the other end said, "Excuse me, but can you tell me, 'what is the meaning of life'?" Needless to say, I didn't have an answer for him that early in the morning, neither do I know if I would have had an answer for him had it been a more reasonable time of day. I have often thought about this occurrence in the decades since. Perhaps it was a missed opportunity to speak truth to someone on the other end of a prank call. What would you say if someone asked you this question, and you only had thirty seconds to answer?

People everywhere are looking for the meaning of life. They want to know there is a purpose for their existence. Many feel insignificant like one small grain of sand on an endless beach. The writer of Ecclesiastes gave his survey of life and the futility of many pursuits people explore, and ultimately said "The conclusion, when all has been heard, is: fear God and keep his commandments, because this applies to every person" (Eccle. 12:13).

Jesus said it this way "The thief comes only to steal and kill and destroy; I came that they may have life, and have it abundantly" (John 10:10). There are many forces in life that can steal your joy, kill your happiness, and destroy your very essence. That is what the forces of evil do, and these forces do not care about you. That is not who Jesus is. He is the opposite of those forces. He is a force for life and abundant life at that, a life beyond your expectations. Jesus came and sacrificially gave Himself for "the sheep" (John 10:11) so you could experience the best of what God has to offer. The gospel of John chapter 10 details all this for you.

The *Westminster Shorter Catechism* explains the meaning of life this way, "Q. What is the chief end of man? A. Man's chief end is to glorify God and to enjoy him forever."[59] Truly, our purpose, as redeemed followers of Christ, is to glorify God in all we say and do. The second part of the answer to the catechism question is just as important as the first. God wants us to delight in Him, to enjoy who He is and all the good gifts He provides. It was the great Olympic runner and Christian missionary Eric Liddell who famously said, "God made me fast. And when I run, I feel His pleasure."[60] God made you,

---

[59] The Westminster Shorter Catechism, d-scatechism.pdf, accessed December 15, 2019, https://bpc.org/wp-content/uploads/2015/06/d-scatechism.pdf.

[60] Quotes, Goodreads, accessed December 15, 2019, https://www.goodreads.com/author/quotes/802465.Eric_Liddell.

too, and He gifted you just like he gifted Eric Liddell. How will you use those gifts to enjoy God? Enjoy the rest of your life pursuing God's plan and purposes for you. I wish you Godspeed on your journey, and I hope to see you at the end of the trail!

ABOUT THE AUTHOR

Stan Blades is an ordinary guy with an extraordinary God. He has been blessed with a loving wife and two talented sons. Stan is a lifelong educator and is currently a worship pastor, as well.

CPSIA information can be obtained
at www.ICGtesting.com
Printed in the USA
JSHW041126150421
13594JS00001B/70